Series / Number 07-041

GAME THEORY
Concepts and
Applications

FRANK C. ZAGARE
Boston University

SAGE PUBLICATIONS
The International Professional Publishers
Newbury Park   London   New Delhi

For information address:

SAGE Publications, Inc.
2455 Teller Road
Newbury Park, California 91320
E-mail: order@sagepub.com

SAGE Publications Ltd.
6 Bonhill Street
London EC2A 4PU
United Kingdom

SAGE Publications India Pvt. Ltd.
M-32 Market
Greater Kailash I
New Delhi 110 048 India

International Standard Book Number 0-8039-2050-4

Library of Congress Catalog Card No. L.C. 83-051821

QA 269. ZAG.

97   98   99   00   01   02   03   15   14   13   12   11   10   09

When citing a professional paper, please use the proper form. Remember to cite the correct Sage
University Paper series title and include the paper number. One of the two following formats can
be adapted (depending on the style manual used):

(1) IVERSEN, GUDMUND R. and NORPOTH, HELMUT (1976) "Analysis of Variance." Sage
University Paper series on Quantitative Applications in the Social Sciences, 07-001. Beverly
Hills and London: Sage Publications.

OR

(2) Iversen, Gudmund R. and Norpoth, Helmut. 1976. *Analysis of Variance.* Sage University Paper
series on Quantitative Applications in the Social Sciences, series no. 07-001. Beverly Hills
and London: Sage Publications.

CONTENTS

To my own personal V-solution:
(D. J., Jen, Tish, Catherine, Ann)
A uniqueness theorem is easily demonstrated.

Series Editor's Introduction

Though at one time game theory may have been viewed as the esoteric subject matter of mathematical specialists, its concepts and terminology now pervade much of our thinking in the social sciences. The idea of rational behavior, for example, owes much to the notion of selecting optimal strategies in gamelike situations. The notion of a Prisoners' Dilemma has found applications in nearly every field of each of the social sciences. And the now huge literature on social choice can trace many of its roots to game theory.

Because of this extensive use of its fundamental components, Frank C. Zagare's *Game Theory: Concepts and Applications* should be useful to a wide audience. The volume requires only a background in high school mathematics. Yet through careful exposition, Zagare is able to convey the major divisions of game theory in a way that is clear, precise, and readily understood. Frequent examples give the reader an immediate idea of how many of the concepts and results have been applied in analyzing everyday situations. If you have heard of zero-sum games, mixed strategies, Prisoners' Dilemmas, and minimax strategies, but feel that you should know more about these topics, Zagare's introduction will add greatly to your understanding of many aspects of modern social science.

—*Richard G. Niemi*
Series Co-editor

Introduction

Game theory is formally a branch of mathematics developed to deal with conflict of interest situations in social science. Although the origins of the theory can be traced to early articles in the 1920s by mathematicians Emile Borel (1921, 1924) and John von Neumann (1928), the field was only definitely established when von Neumann and economist Oskar Morgenstern published *Theory of Games and Economic Behavior* (1944[1953]). Hailed as one of the major scientific achievements of the twentieth century, this book remains the seminal work in the field.

Game theory is not, strictly speaking, about games—at least, not the way most people think of games—although the interactive process that characterizes most games—be they card games, board games, athletic games, or other types—is certainly part of the subject matter of game theory. When game theorists use the word "game," they are referring to any social situation involving two or more actors (players) in which the interests of the players are interconnected or interdependent. Thus, while poker, parchisi, and prize fighting are all types of games, so are wage bargaining situations, arms races, or even war. Games, therefore, may be lighthearted, especially when the stakes are small, but they may also involve serious business.

Underlying the entire structure of game theory is the key assumption that players in a game are *rational* (or *utility maximizers*). As game theorists use this term, rationality simply means that a player in an interactive situation will act to bring about the most preferred of the possible outcomes, given the constraint that other players are also acting in the same way.

As a theory of rational decision making, game theory is thought by some to be primarily a type of *normative theory* (see, for instance, Rapoport, 1958), that specifies how players should act if they are to achieve their goals. Indeed, it is, and has been frequently used as a normative device, especially by military planners to solve difficult

AUTHOR'S NOTE: *I would like to thank Steven J. Brams, who read an earlier version of this essay and made many helpful suggestions; Jacek Kugler, whose particular brand of encouragement made it all much more pleasant; and Suzanne O'Connor, who typed, and retyped, each successive iteration of this monograph.*

tactical or logistical problems. But game theory is much more than a normative theory. Once some of its key assumptions are operationalized and ascribed empirical meaning, game theory can also be considered a *descriptive,* or *positive,* theory, capable of explanation and prediction. As such it has the potential to develop into a fully rigorous, deductive theory of human behavior, be that behavior social, economic, military, or political.

This potential has not been unrecognized by social scientists. Long ago, sociologists, political scientists, and international relations specialists saw the relevance of game theory for studying the processes underlying coalition formation, an important area of concern in each of these disciplines. The enormous experimental gaming literature attests to the significant impact of game-theoretic models in social psychology (Colman, 1982; Hamburger, 1979). And a recent review by Schotter and Schwödiauer (1980) in the *Journal of Economic Literature* demonstrates how deeply the theory of games has penetrated economics since the publication of von Neumann and Morgenstern's monumental work. Indeed, it is virtually impossible to be well versed in any social science today without taking cognizance of the contributions of game theorists. It may even be true, as Nigel Howard (1971: 202) has persuasively argued

> that game theory is becoming a unifying force in the social sciences, encompassing economics, psychology, politics, and history within a single mathematical theory capable of being applied to the understanding of all interactions between conscious beings.

Many, however, remain unconvinced; others lack the requisite skills for adapting, applying, or extending game-theoretic models to their own particular research fields. This essay, therefore, is an attempt to convert the unconverted and initiate the uninitiated. I plan to do this by providing a brief, yet comprehensive, overview of the major divisions of game theory and, in the process, demonstrating the applicability of game-theoretic models for analyzing a wide variety of conflict of interest situations.

To achieve this objective, the subject will be divided into four chapters. In Chapter 1 the rudimentary concepts and principal assumptions of the theory will be discussed, and two devices for abstracting the structure of a game, the extensive and normal form, will be examined. Chapter 2 will consider two-person games of total conflict (zero-sum games) and present the Minimax Theorem, the Fundamental

Theorem of Game Theory. Chapter 3 will investigate the underlying nature of those two-person games in which the players have both conflicting and complementary interest (nonzero-sum games). Finally, Chapter 4 will explore games played by more than two players (n-person games), and the complications introduced when the possibility of coalitions among the players arises.

F. C. Z.

GAME THEORY
Concepts and Applications

FRANK C. ZAGARE
Boston University

1. REPRESENTING GAMES:
EXTENSIVE AND NORMAL FORMS

Primitive Concepts

As previously indicated, game theory is a theory of interdependent choice. Technically, the simplest type of game is a *one-person game,* sometimes called a *game against nature,* wherein a single player makes a decision in the face of an environment assumed to be indifferent or neutral. One-person games, though, have aroused little interest among social theorists for the obvious reason that the most intriguing situations involve at least two players. *Two-person games,* therefore, are the most elementary interactive situations of general concern to social scientists. Games that involve more than two players are called *n-person games.*

In game theory, a *player* can be an individual, or a group of individuals functioning as a decision-making unit. Individuals or groups become players when their decisions, coupled with the decision of at least one other actor, produce an *outcome.* Outcomes may be trivial when the game itself is trivial; outcomes may also involve life and death for millions of people when great nations are linked in a gamelike way.

The options available to players to bring about particular outcomes are called *strategies.* Strategies themselves can be decomposed into a sequence of decisions called *choices,* made at various decision points called *moves.* The selection of a particular strategy from the set of possible strategies by each player is called a *play* of the game. Strategies are linked to outcomes by a mathematical function that specifies the consequences of the various combinations of strategy choices by all of the players in a game.

Players are assumed to be able to evaluate and compare the consequences associated with the set of possible outcomes and assign numbers, called utilities, to each outcome indicating a *preference* relationship among them. When these numbers are judged to reflect only a rank ordering of the outcomes, they are called *ordinal* utilities; when they indicate both order and intensity of preference, they are called *cardinal* utilties.[1]

The Extensive or Game Tree
Form of Representation

In representing games, game theorists seek to abstract the essential features from structurally similar but otherwise different conflict situations. Exactly what constitutes an essential feature depends upon the predilections of the analyst and the structural complexity of the game under examination. But for the two forms discussed in this chapter, the *extensive* and the *normal* forms of representation—used primarily in the analysis of two-person games—the essential features include all of the primitive terms discussed in the previous section namely, the players, their strategies, the possible outcomes, and a preference function for each player over the set of outcomes.[2]

To see how these features can be depicted symbolically, consider for now Figure 1.1, an extensive form of the strategic situation facing American and Japanese military leaders in February 1943, during the critical stage of the struggle for New Guinea, when Allied intelligence detected evidence of a Japanese convoy assembling at the port of Rabaul, in the nearby island of New Britain, for the purpose of reinforcing the Japanese position in New Guinea (Haywood, 1954). The symbolic device used in Figure 1.1 to construct the extensive form representation of the Battle of the Bismarck Sea is called a *game tree*. Formally, a game tree is a collection of points, called *nodes or vertices*, that are connected to each other by lines that are termed *branches*. Each node on the tree represents a point of decision (i.e., a move), and each branch represents the choices available to a particular player at that move.

This game tree is constructed to be read from bottom to top, with the bottom node indicating the player with the first move. For instance, in Figure 1.1, since the Japanese are arbitrarily assumed to move first, the bottom node is assigned to them. The two branches emanating from this node represent the choices available to the Japanese for routing their convoy from Rabaul to New Guinea, a trip that was estimated to require three days. The Japanese could either send their transport ships around the northern part of New Britain, where rain and poor visibility were

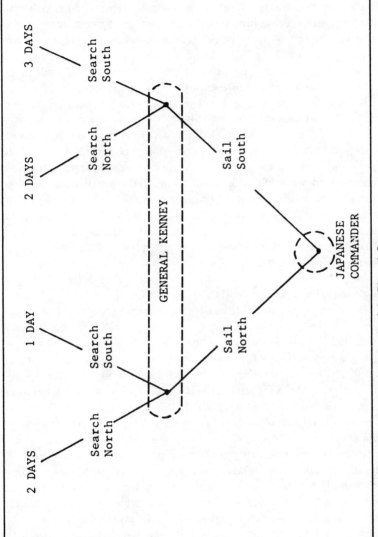

Figure 1.1 Extensive-Form Representation of the Battle of the Bismark Sea

13

predicted, or sail their ships along the southern part of the island, where clear weather was expected.

For his part, the commander of the Allied Air Force in the Southwest Pacific, General George Kenney, enjoined by General MacArthur to intercept and inflict maximum destruction on the Japanese convoy, also had two choices. Kenney could concentrate the bulk of his reconnaissance aircraft along either the northern or the southern part of New Britain. This is indicated by the two branches found at each node at the end of the two branches representing the Japanese choices.

The dotted lines enclosing the moves of both the Japanese commander and General Kenney are called *information sets*. Information sets are used to represent each player's knowledge of his or her place on the tree and, hence, the information available to that player about the choices made by other players at previous moves. As the information sets are drawn in Figure 1.1, they reveal that Kenney did not know whether the Japanese had sailed north or south when he made his choice. This is indicated by the inclusion of two moves within his information set. By contrast, since the Japanese are assumed to have made the first choice, they obviously could determine their place on the tree when it was their turn to move, though they could have no information about prior choices because it was assumed that there were no prior choices. Hence, there is only a single move enclosed within the Japanese information set.

When all players are able to determine their exact locations on the game tree at every move, that is, when each information set contains a single move, a game is said to be characterized by *perfect information*. In a game of perfect information, then, each player is fully informed about all prior choices when it is his or her turn to move. Clearly, since this is not the case in Figure 1.1, the Battle of the Bismarck Sea was not a game of perfect information. Neither the Japanese nor the American command had foreknowledge of the other's choice when they made their own choices.

Related to, but distinct from, the concept of perfect information is the idea of *complete information*. Briefly, players with complete information know both the rules of the game (to be defined below) and the preferences of the other players over the set of outcomes. Unless otherwise noted, complete information will be assumed throughout this essay, even though it rarely exists in the real world, since it provides a useful starting point for examining games. Like all assumptions made by game theorists, however, the complete information assumption can be relaxed or modified to take into account the exigencies of the situation being modeled.

The possible outcomes of this game, resulting from the different combinations of choices of the players, are indicated at each end point of the game tree. In this case the outcomes are estimates provided Kenney by his staff of the number of days he would have to bomb the Japanese convoy after it was sighted by his reconnaissance aircraft. (For the details of these estimates, see Haywood [1954].) The set of possible outcomes, when coupled with the other details contained on the game tree, that is, an enumeration of the choices available to each player at each move and information sets indicating each player's ability to determine his or her location on the tree at each move, constitute the *rules of the game.*

What were the preferences of the players regarding the possible outcomes of this game? Since Kenney obviously preferred, and was so ordered, to maximize the number of days his forces could bomb the Japanese, it seems safe to assume that he preferred the outcomes in the order of their magnitude; and since the Japanese commander clearly preferred to minimize the convoy's exposure to Kenney's bombers, it can be assumed that his rank ordering of the outcomes was inversely related to their magnitude. Thus, the best outcome for Kenney was the worst for the Japanese, the next-best for Kenney was the next-worst for the Japanese, and so on.

Games like the Battle of the Bismarck Sea, in which the players have diametrically opposed interests, are known as *strictly competitive* games. If in a strictly competitive game the preferences (or payoffs) of the players are measured on a cardinal scale, and the payoffs sum to some constant, the game is termed *constant-sum.* If the constant is zero, the game is called a *zero-sum* game. Since all constant-sum games can be transformed into a zero-sum game by the addition or subtraction of an appropriate constant from the payoffs of the players, constant-sum and zero-sum games are strategically equivalent. For purposes of exposition, it will be assumed that the Japanese commander's cardinal utility scale was the reverse of General Kenney's. With this assumption, the Battle of the Bismarck Sea can be considered a zero-sum game.

Taken together, the preferences of each player *and* the elements summarized under the rubric "rules of the game" (see above) are said to constitute a game in *extensive,* or *game tree,* form. Thus, two interactive situations, with identical rules but played by players who evaluate the outcomes differently, are considered distinct games. Conversely, when two different sets of players are involved in separate interactions with the same set of rules, and have identical preference patterns, they are considered to be playing the same game.

The Normal or Matrix
Form of Representation

The second device developed to abstract the interactive conditions that define a game is called the *normal,* or *matrix,* form of representation. The normal form rests upon the notion of a (pure) strategy, which may be thought of as a complete contingency plan that specifies a particular choice for a player in every situation that might arise in a game.[3] For instance, in the Battle of the Bismarck Sea, the Japanese had two strategies, corresponding (in this case) to their two choices, either sailing north or sailing south. Similarly, since General Kenney's two moves are contained within a single information set and, hence, are indistinguishable to him, his two strategies are the same as the two choices available to him, that is, either to search north or to search south.

Although it may not always be so easy to identify all of the strategies available to a player, it is theoretically possible to do this for every game.[4] Assuming, then, that the set of logically possible strategies for each player can be identified, every finite game[5] represented in extensive form can be transformed into a game depicted in normal form, in which each player has exactly one move, that is, a choice of one strategy from among the set of available strategies.

To illustrate the connections between these two different methods of abstraction, consider now Figure 1.2, the normal form representation of the Battle of the Bismarck Sea. In this representation General Kenney's two strategies have been arbitrarily assigned to the rows of this matrix, while the Japanese commander's strategies have been assigned to the columns. By convention, in a zero-sum game the entry in each cell of the matrix contains the row player's (here, Kenney's) evaluation of the outcome associated with the choice of the corresponding strategies. For example, the outcome "3 days" of bombing, found at the intersection of Kenney's search south strategy and the Japanese commander's sail south strategy, represents the payoff to Kenney should these two strategies be chosen. This is the same payoff found at the endpoint of the game tree of Figure 1.1 associated with the corresponding choices of the two players.

Since it may have been obscured by the simplicity of the preceding example, it should be pointed out that a good deal of the descriptive richness of the extensive form is lost when a game is represented in normal form. Game theorists have accepted this loss of detail because the normal form has proven to be a very useful conceptual device for examining entire categories of games. Indeed, without the development

JAPANESE COMMANDER:

		SAIL NORTH	SAIL SOUTH
GENERAL KENNEY:	SEARCH NORTH	2 days	2 days
	SEARCH SOUTH	1 day	3 days

SOURCE: O. G. Haywood, Jr., "Military Decision and Game Theory," Vol. 2 (November 1954), pp. 365-385, **Operations Research.** Copyright © 1954 by the Operations Research Society of America. Reprinted by permission.

Figure 1.2 Normal-Form Representation of the Battle of the Bismark Sea

of what Luce and Raiffa (1957: 55) call a "radical conceptual simplification," it is almost certain that the maturation of modern game theory would have been severely retarded. It is precisely for this reason that Shubik (1982: 68) has argued that the primary virtue of the normal form is that it is "deliberately nondescriptive."

Because almost all of the analysis in the next two chapters will take a normal form representation as its starting point, it is important to be as explicit as possible about what is being abstracted away when a game is depicted in this way. For one thing, the normal form does not specify the information structure of a game. It may be impossible to tell from the normal form alone whether a game is one of perfect or imperfect information. Second, information about the sequence of moves and countermoves is lost in a normal form representation. Consequently, while it is always possible to transform every finite game in extensive form into a game in normal form, the converse is not true.

This loss of information about the sequence of moves, however, should not be interpreted to mean that the normal form is completely "timeless," as Young (1975: 314) has suggested. The normal form can be used to capture the dynamics of both simultaneous strategy choices, as in Figure 1.2, and of sequential strategy choices, as the following example of a game played by American and Israeli decision makers in 1967 will illustrate.

Representing Games:
The 1967 Middle East Crisis

This particular game was precipitated on May 22, 1967, when Egyptian President Nasser ordered the Strait of Tiran closed to Israeli shipping. After Nasser closed the strait, the Israeli leadership quickly concluded that they would have to either (1) submit to his attempted *fait accompli,* or (2) resist Egypt by using force to reopen the strait.

United States decision makers were also faced with a difficult choice at this time. Like the Israelis, American leaders also seriously considered two different courses of action. They had to decide whether to (1) withhold (W) full political support of Israel's demand that the strait be reopened immediately, or (2) back (B) Israel by either taking or supporting action designed to reopen the strait. Linking the United States and Israel in a high-stakes game was the simple fact that the leaders of both states saw their interests and objectives in this crisis being affected not only by their own choice but also by the choice of the other.

The options available to the United States and Israeli leaders, and the outcomes associated with them, are summarized in the game tree of Figure 1.3. Since, empirically, the Israelis had to move first, the first node, necessarily enclosed alone in an information set, is assigned to Israel. And since United States decision makers made their choice after Israel, and in full cognizance of the Israeli choice, each of the two moves available to the United States are also enclosed alone in an information set. Unlike the Battle of the Bismarck Sea, then, this was a game of perfect information.

The reader will notice that at the endpoint of each branch of the game tree is an ordered pair that represents the ranking of each outcome by the player with the first choice (here, Israel) and the player with the second choice (here, the United States), respectively. Two numbers are used in this example to indicate the preferences of the players because the interests of the players were not diametrically opposed. Consequently, the payoffs of the player with the second choice cannot be inferred from the payoffs of the player with the first choice, as is the case in zero-sum games like the Battle of the Bismarck Sea. In other words, this was a nonzero-sum game.

In Figure 1.3, the outcomes are ranked from highest to lowest, with "4" assigned to each player's best outcome, "3" assigned to each player's next-best outcome, and so on. For example, the outcome associated with an American decision to back Israel should Israel decide to resist Nasser, (4,3), is assumed to be Israel's best outcome and the next-best outcome for the United States. (The preference rankings of outcomes in a game are not necessarily self-evident. For the details supporting this particular ranking, see Zagare [1981].)

The structural differences for the normal form implied by the sequential choices made in this game are readily observed by considering Figure 1.4. As before, the two choices of the player with the first move

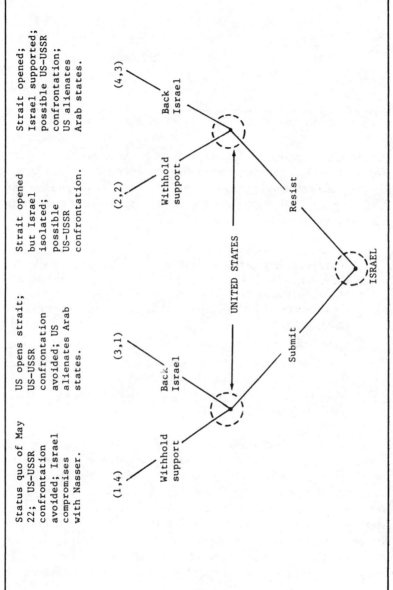

Figure 3.1 Extensive-Form Representative of the June American-Israeli Game

Status quo of May 22; US-USSR confrontation avoided; Israel compromises with Nasser.

US opens strait; US-USSR confrontation avoided; US alienates Arab states.

Strait opened but Israel isolated; possible US-USSR confrontation.

Strait opened; Israel supported; possible US-USSR confrontation; US alienates Arab states.

(1,4) Withhold support

(3,1) Back Israel

UNITED STATES

(2,2) Withhold support

(4,3) Back Israel

Submit

Resist

ISRAEL

19

		UNITED STATES:			
		W/W	B/B	W/B	B/W
ISRAEL:	SUBMIT	(1,4)	(3,1)	(1,4)	(3,1)
	RESIST	(2,2)	(4,3)	(4,3)	(2,2)

Figure 1.4   Normal-Form Representation of the June 1967 American-Israeli Game

(i.e., Israel) can be directly translated into strategies. But this is not the case for the player choosing second (i.e., the United States). Since the United States has two choices for each of the two choices of Israel, it has $2 \times 2 = 4$ possible strategies. More specifically, the United States could select any one of the following sets of options.

(1)   Withhold support of Israel regardless of Israel's choice. This strategy can be represented in shorthand by the notation (W/W); the letter to the left of the slash indicates the U.S. response to Israel's first strategy (i.e., submit), and the letter to the right of the slash indicates the U.S. response to Israel's second strategy (i.e., resist).

(2)   Back Israel regardless of Israel's choice—(B/B).

(3)   Withhold support if Israel submits and back Israel if Israel resists—(W/B). Call this strategy tat-for-tit.

(4)   Back Israel if Israel submits and withhold support if Israel resists—(B/W). Call this strategy tit-for-tat.

Israel's two strategies, and the four strategies of the United States, give rise to eight possible outcomes in the normal form representation of this game. As before, these outcomes can be read directly from the game tree. For example, suppose that the Israeli leadership decided to resist Nasser and American policy makers decided upon a tat-for-tit strategy. Since the American tat-for-tit strategy implies support for Israeli resistance, the outcome found in the cell associated with these two strategies, i.e., (4,3), is the same as the outcome found at the endpoint of the game tree associated with the corresponding choices.

Concluding Comments

Translating the amorphous structure of the real world into a game model is an exercise that may be neither straightforward nor intuitively obvious. For the social scientist the conceptual problems associated with this task may pose the single most difficult stumbling block for the fruitful application of the theoretical apparatus of the theory of games. But for the game theorist qua game theorist, the practical difficulties involved in bringing the salient concepts of an abstract, formal model into an isomorphic relationship with empirical reality constitutes a subsidiary problem. Game theorists take the structure of a game as given. For them the principal problem to be solved involves the specification of a *solution* for each recognizable category of games. For games represented in normal form, a solution consists of the identification of an optimal strategy for each player—to be defined shortly—and of the outcome that rational players will choose.

As will be seen in subsequent chapters, not all games have agreed-upon solutions. In general, as games become more complex, that is, as more players are added to a game and as some simplifying assumptions are relaxed, solution concepts become more numerous and agreement among theorists about what constitutes a solution for a particular category of games becomes less common.

This lack of consensus, however, is not the case for one particular class of games—namely, the general, finite, two-person zero-sum game. Game theorists, uncharacteristically, are in almost unanimous agreement about what strategy is optimal and what outcome should be chosen by rational players in a zero-sum game. This solution, neatly summarized by von Neumann's famous Minimax Theorem, is the subject of the next chapter.

2. ZERO-SUM GAMES: CONFLICT AT THE EXTREME

Introduction

In this chapter, zero-sum games, which are games of total conflict, will be examined. In these games, value is neither created nor destroyed. What one player wins, the other loses, and vice versa. Hence, zero-sum games represent interdependent choice at one extreme, the extreme of diametrically opposed interests.

While game theorists are more or less in agreement with respect to their prescriptions for this category of games, there is also considerable skepticism among some social scientists about the empirical relevance of zero-sum games. Recall from Chapter 1 that for a game to be considered zero-sum, the preferences of the players must be exactly the opposite.

Given this restrictive requirement, it is possibly true, as Snyder and Diesing (1977: 38) argue, that "the zero-sum game is not to be found empirically in international relations," and Bacharach (1977: 60) is probably correct in his judgment that the existence of a zero-sum game in the real world is a "sheer fluke." In almost any gamelike situation, it is not hard to imagine some area of common interest among players. Even in war, the most extreme form of human conflict, nations may have a shared interest in limiting the scope of hostilities.

On the other hand, the relative rarity of a zero-sum game in its pure form does not mean that they are devoid of relevance for social scientists. Consider, for instance, two politicians competing for one office, or two corporations competing for a single contract, or two nations competing for the support of a third. While the players in each of these hypothetical situations might have some interests in common—if only the continued existence of the political, social, or economic system that made their competition possible in the first place—it is clear that the most salient aspect of each of these conflicts is the zero-sum component. Thus, as Riker (1962b: 31) has argued, in games like these, "which are perceived as requiring indivisible victory, the zero-sum model is probably best."

Zero-Sum Games with a Saddlepoint

Whether or not zero-sum games occur with any recognizable frequency in the real world is an empirical question whose answer, unfortunately, lies outside the scope of this book. In this and the next section, attention will be confined to the theoretical problem of specifying a solution for these games, whatever their empirical relevance may be.

To this end, consider for now the strategic situation facing the leadership of the Dual Alliance of Austria and Germany and of the Franco-Russian coalition in July 1914. At this time Serbia, a Russian ally, had just rejected an Austrian ultimatum demanding, *inter alia*, that Austria be permitted to conduct an investigation within Serbia of the plot of some Serbian nationalists to assassinate the heir to the throne of Austria-Hungary. In the wake of the Serbian rejection, Austria and Germany, considered a single player because of their alliance, had to decide whether to attempt some sort of compromise with Serbia which, after all, had accepted some elements of the original ultimatum, or to carry out their threat to use force to wipe out the subversive movement within Serbia. For their part, Russia and France, also considered a single player because of their common interest in limiting Austrian influence in the Balkans, had to decide whether to back away from the

| | RUSSIA–FRANCE: | | |
	DESERT SERBIA	BACK SERBIA	Minimum of rows
COMPROMISE	A. Compromise with Serbia; some Russian influence in Serbia preserved. (2)	C. Serbia saved; Russian influence in Balkans preserved; continued Serbian agitation; Austrian Empire begins to disintegrate. (1)	1
DUAL ALLIANCE (AUSTRIA–GERMANY):			
ATTACK	B. Russia humiliated and loses influence in Balkans; Austria gains control of Serbia and preserves Empire. (4)	D. War. (3)	③
Maximum of columns	4	③	

Figure 2.1 Normal-Form Representation of the July 1914 Crisis in Europe

SOURCE: Glenn H. Snyder and Paul Diesing, **Conflict Among Nations: Bargaining, Decision Making, and System Structure in International Crisis**, Fig. 2-28, p. 94. Copyright © 1977 by Princeton University Press. Reprinted by permission.

Russian promise to support Serbia, or to mobilize their forces and demonstrate their intention to stand alongside Serbia.

The four outcomes, associated with the possible strategy choices of the two players (coalitions), are summarized verbally in Figure 2.1. According to Snyder and Diesing (1977: 94), who suggested this representation of the 1914 crisis, the preferences of the players were exactly the opposite of one another, making this a zero-sum game.

In the outcome matrix of Figure 2.1, the most-preferred outcome of the row player (here, the Dual Alliance) is represented by "4," its second most-preferred outcome by "3," and so on. Since the preference scale of the column player (here, Russia and France) is assumed to be the opposite of the Dual Alliance's, and hence can be inferred from it, it is not represented.

On what basis should a player select a strategy in zero-sum games like this one? Although there are many strategic principles that could be evoked (for a discussion, see Colman, 1982: Chap. 2), theorists are in general agreement that the *maximin* principle, which essentially requires that players maximize their *security level* (to be defined presently), is the soundest.

To determine each player's best strategy, then, notice first that if the Dual Alliance chooses its compromise strategy, the worst outcome that could result is outcome C, its least preferred (with a payoff of 1) while the Dual Alliance could assure itself at least its second most-preferred outcome D, (with a payoff of 3), if it chooses its attack strategy. Define the worst outcome associated with each strategy as the security level of that strategy. The security level of each of the Dual Alliance's two strategies—that is, the minimum entry in each row—is indicated to the right of the outcome matrix of Figure 2.1.

It is easy to see that the security level of the Dual Alliance's attack strategy (i.e., 3) is higher than the security level of its compromise strategy (i.e., 1). Thus, to maximize its security level, the Dual Alliance should attack. Since this strategy is associated with the outcome that is the maximum of the minimum entry in each row, it is called a *maximin* strategy.

The security level for each strategy of Russia-France is listed just below Figure 2.1. Recall that the interests of the players in this game were diametrically opposed. Thus, the higher payoff to the Dual Alliance, the lower the payoff to Russia-France. Consequently, the security level for each strategy of the Russian-French coalition corresponds to the highest entry in each column, that is, to the column maximum. For instance, the worst outcome associated with its desert Serbia strategy is its least-preferred outcome, B (i.e., 4), and the worst outcome associated with its back Serbia strategy is its third most-preferred outcome, D (i.e., 3). Therefore, in order to maximize its security level, the Russian-French coalition should back Serbia. Since this choice entails choosing a strategy associated with the minimum of the column maxima, it is called a *minimax* strategy.

Notice that the maximin and minimax strategies of the two players are associated with the same outcome (i.e., the value 3, which is circled) in Figure 2.1. When this occurs, the maximin and minimax strategies are said to be in equilibrium, and the outcome associated with them is called an *equilibrium* outcome or a *saddlepoint*. When two strategies are in equilibrium (and hence produce an equilibrium outcome), neither player has an incentive unilaterally to change its strategy. For instance, if the Dual Alliance should switch from its attack strategy to its compromise strategy, it would induce its worst outcome, 1, rather than its next-best outcome, 3, while a unilateral strategy switch by the Russian-French coalition from its back Serbia to its desert Serbia strategy would change the outcome from its next-worst, 3, to its worst, 4.

In zero-sum games with a saddlepoint, strategies associated with a saddlepoint are considered *optimal* and players who choose these strategies are termed *rational*. There are a number of reasons for this.

First, equilibrium strategies secure for each player the *value* of the game—that is, the best outcome that either player can assure itself of against a rational opponent. (In a game with a saddlepoint, the value of the game is always equal to the utility of the saddlepoint.) Second, as just illustrated, these strategies maximize each player's security level. Finally, equilibrium strategies, when they exist, are the best response to the strategy that maximizes the other player's security level. For example, if the Dual Alliance had been able to determine that the Russian-French coalition was going to choose the strategy that maximized its security level (i.e., its minimax strategy of backing Serbia), its best response would be to choose the strategy that maximized its own security level (i.e., its maximin attack strategy). And if the Russian-French coalition knew that the Dual Alliance was going to choose its maximin strategy, its best response would be its minimax strategy. Stated differently, in games with a saddlepoint, if a player has advance information that its opponent plans to choose its optimal strategy, it is not helped by this knowledge, nor is its opponent hurt. The optimal strategy is the same with or without this knowledge. In a way, then, zero-sum games with a saddlepoint are *strictly determined,* and they are sometimes identified by this label.

Both players, of course, chose their equilibrium strategies in the 1914 crisis game, and in the process precipitated a world war. While this outcome cannot be considered satisfactory by any reasonable standard, the strategies that brought it about were optimal, and game-theoretically sound, in the sense that they were the best choices either side could make, given the structure of the game they played. Needless to say, had either side been able to foresee the consequences of their action (both coalitions believed that the war would remain localized and limited in scope and duration) they might have evaluated the outcomes differently and been able to avoid war.

Like their counterparts in the 1914 crisis, both commanders in the Battle of the Bismarck Sea also chose their maximin and minimax strategies associated with the unique equilibrium outcome in that game, and thereby maximized their respective security levels (see Figure 1.2). General Kenney concentrated the bulk of his reconnaissance aircraft along the northern part of New Britain, while the Japanese commander decided to route his convoy along the northern route. Consequently, the Japanese convoy was subjected to two days of bombing. (Readers should convince themselves that Kenney's search north strategy was a maximin strategy, that the Japanese sail north strategy was a minimax strategy, and that the outcome associated with these two strategies is the only equilibrium outcome in this game.) Unbeknownst to the Japanese, however, Kenney had modified a number of his aircraft for low-level bombing, thereby inflicting unusually heavy losses on the Japanese convoy.

Still, as Haywood (1954: 369) points out, one cannot say that "the Japanese commander erred in his decision," though one might argue that the disastrous defeat of the Japanese forces resulted from a failure of Japanese intelligence to detect Kenney's new bombing technique (Brams, 1975: 8). Had the Japanese sailed south, and Kenney chosen his maximin strategy of searching north, the result would have been the same—two days of bombing. But if the Japanese had sailed south and Kenney searched south, the Japanese convoy would have been exposed to Kenney's bombers for an even longer period of time—three days. Thus, the Japanese minimax strategy of sailing north was an optimal choice against Kenney's maximin strategy, and was also a better choice than their nonminimax strategy should Kenney have departed from his own maximin strategy.

Equilibrium outcomes, when they exist, and the optimal strategies associated with them, are not difficult to identify. One method of identification, as just illustrated, is to locate the strategy that maximizes each player's security level. When these strategies are both associated with the same outcome, the outcome is an equilibrium. When they are different, there is no saddlepoint in the game and at least one player has an incentive, unilaterally, to change to another strategy, as will be demonstrated in the next section.

A simpler and more efficient search procedure exists, however, for identifying an equilibrium outcome. Provided that only the row player's payoffs are represented in the payoff matrix, it is not difficult to show that an equilibrium outcome exists in a zero-sum game if and only if there is an outcome that is simultaneously *the minimum of its row and the maximum of its column*. When this test is satisfied, the row player's maximin strategy and the column player's minimax strategy are associated with the same outcome, and the game is strictly determined. (Readers should determine that the outcome identified as the equilibrium in the Battle of the Bismarck Sea and the 1914 crisis game satisfy this requirement.)

To summarize briefly, there are two good reasons why players in a zero-sum game should choose a strategy associated with an equilibrium outcome. First, such a strategy maximizes a player's security level and guarantees at least the value of the game; second, an equilibrium strategy is the best counterchoice to the strategy that maximizes the other player's security level. To be sure, this prescription is rather conservative. It is predicated upon the principle that players should attempt to foreclose the possibility of their least-preferred outcomes occurring, rather than attempting to bring about their most-preferred outcomes, when there is a conflict between these two objectives. But in defense of this prescription, it is worth pointing out that the choice of an equilibrium strategy is consistent with the conventional military doctrine of the United States (especially apropos for the analysis of a zero-sum game) which enjoins commanders to select a strategy in view of what an opponent is able to do (i.e., capabilities) rather than in view of what it is going to do (i.e., intentions).[6] As Haywood (1954:370) has argued, the similarity between this military rule of thumb and the prescription to choose an equilibrium strategy in a zero-sum game is no "mere coincidence."

In addition to the arguments just cited to justify the selection of equilibrium strategies in zero-sum games, equilibrium outcomes, and the maximin and minimax strategies associated with them, possess two other characteristics that make them particularly appealing as the foundation for a solution concept for this category of games. First, although equilibria are not necessarily unique, when more than one equilibrium outcome exists, each equilibrium is *equivalent,* that is, has the same value. This means that from the point of view of the players, there is no necessary tension among various equilibria when multiple equilibria exist in a zero-sum game. Second, equilibrium strategies are *interchangeable* in those games containing more than one saddlepoint. This means that an equilibrium outcome is found at the intersection of all equilibrium strategies in these games. Therefore, regardless of which equilibrium strategy a player selects, the outcome will be a saddlepoint if the other player also selects some equilibrium strategy. As will be seen in Chapter 3, the fact that equilibrium outcomes are not necessarily equivalent nor interchangeable in nonzero-sum games poses some problems for the construction of a general solution concept for these games.

To conclude this section, one theorem will be noted, but not proved— the *Perfect Information Theorem*-about two-person zero-sum games. Recall that a game is characterized by perfect information if each information set on a game tree contains a single move. It is not difficult to show that every two-person, finite, zero-sum game of perfect information is strictly determined, that is, contains a saddlepoint (Zermelo, 1912).

With regard to this theorem, it is important to note that perfect information is a sufficient, though not a necessary, condition for a game to be strictly determined. To see this, recall that the Battle of the Bismarck Sea was not a game of perfect information, yet it had a saddlepoint and was therefore strictly determined.

Zero-Sum Games Without a Saddlepoint

In the previous section it was argued that a player in a zero-sum game should choose a strategy associated with an equilibrium outcome. But, as will be illustrated shortly, equilibrium outcomes do not exist in all zero-sum games. What strategy, then, is optimal for a player in a zero-sum game without a saddlepoint?

To answer this question, consider another World War II game, called the Battle of Avranches-Gap, played in August 1944 just after the invasion of Normandy. This particular game evolved when Allied forces, under the command of General Omar Bradley, broke out of their beachhead at Avranches through a narrow gap and exposed the west flank of the German Ninth Army, commanded by General von Kluge.

With the Ninth Army in a precarious position, von Kluge had to make a quick decision. As Haywood (1954) reports, he had two logical options. He could either attack the Allied position at Avranches, thereby protecting his west flank, and possibly separating the U.S. Third Army in the south from the U.S. First Army north of Avranches, or he could withdraw eastward to a more defensible position near the Seine River.

Bradley, as reported in his memoirs, considered three strategies, each of which concerned the placement of four divisions he had not yet committed to battle. Bradley could either order his reserves back to reinforce the gap, order them to attack eastward to make a German defensive withdrawal more difficult, or delay and do nothing until the next day.

Depending on which strategies the two generals selected, one of six battles, summarized in Figure 2.2, could be expected to occur. These outcomes, numbered from one to six, indicate Bradley's reported preference ranking among them. Bradley's best outcome is indicated by "6," his next-best outcome by "5," and so on. Presumably, von Kluge's rank ordering of the six outcomes were the reverse of Bradley's. *Assuming that these numbers can also be interpreted to indicate each player's cardinal evaluation of the outcomes,* then the Battle of Avranches-Gap can be analyzed as a zero-sum game.

Before identifying each player's optimal strategy, it should be pointed out that there is one strategy that Bradley should *not* choose under any circumstances. More specifically, Bradley should not reinforce the gap

GENERAL VON KLUGE:

GENERAL BRADLEY:	ATTACK	WITHDRAW
REINFORCE GAP	A. US forces would repel attack; gap holds. (2)	D. US forces deployed for attack that does not come; weak pressure on German withdrawal. (3)
MOVE EASTWARD	B. Germans may break through to cut gap and isolate US Third Army. (1)	E. US forces ideally deployed for harrassment of German retreat; Strong pressure on German withdrawal. (5)
DELAY DECISION	C. Gap holds since reinforcements would be available if needed; if not, they could move east toward the German rear and possibly encircle the German Ninth Army. (6)	F. Reserves one day late in starting eastward to harass German retreat; moderate pressure on German withdrawal. (4)

SOURCE: O. G. Haywood, Jr., "Military Decision and Game Theory," Vol. 2 (November 1954), pp. 365-385, Operations Research. Copyright © 1954 by the Operations Research Society of America. Reprinted by permission.

Figure 2.2 Normal-Form Representation of the Battle of Avranches-Gap

since his delay strategy provides him with a better outcome, regardless of the strategy chosen by von Kluge. For example, if von Kluge attacks, Bradley induces his best outcome, 6, if he delays, and his next-worst outcome, 2, if he reinforces the gap; and if von Kluge withdraws, Bradley induces his third-best outcome, 4, by delaying, his third-worst outcome, 3, by reinforcing the gap.

Technically, Bradley's delay strategy is said to *dominate* his reinforce strategy. More formally, one strategy dominates another strategy if it provides at least as good an outcome in every contingency, and a better outcome in one or more contingencies, than the other strategy. Because it induces a better outcome for him in *every* contingency, Bradley's delay strategy is said to *strictly dominate* his reinforce strategy.[7]

A dominant strategy is unconditionally better than a dominated strategy. It seems safe to assume, then, that a player, if rational, will not select a dominated strategy, and that the search for an optimal strategy can confidently be limited to each player's set of undominated strategies. Accordingly, in Figure 2.3, a reduced version of the Battle of Avranches-Gap is provided, listing only the undominated strategies of the two players and Bradley's evaluation of the associated outcomes.

The question remains: What strategy should each player choose? Each could choose the (pure) strategy[8] that maximizes his security level, but these strategies are not in equilibrium, as is easily demonstrated. In this game, Bradley maximizes his security level and guarantees a payoff of at least 4 by delaying his decision, while von Kluge maximizes his security level and guarantees a payoff of at least 5 by withdrawing. However, Bradley's best counterchoice to von Kluge's withdraw strategy is not his delay strategy but his move eastward strategy, which induces his second highest payoff, 5. Bradley's incentive to switch from his delay strategy to his move eastward strategy, should von Kluge withdraw, is indicated by the arrow from the outcome with a payoff of 4 to the outcome with a payoff of 5 in Figure 2.3.

That the strategies that maximize each player's security level are not equilibrium strategies is also indicated by the fact that they are not associated with the same outcome, as was the case in the 1914 crisis game and the Battle of the Bismarck Sea. This means that the Battle of Avranches-Gap is a zero-sum game without a saddlepoint: There is no entry in the payoff matrix that is simultaneously the minimum entry of its row and the maximum entry of its column. At least one player has a unilateral incentive to switch to another strategy at every outcome, as revealed by the remaining arrows in Figure 2.3. (The vertical arrows indicate Bradley's incentive to move from the outcomes with payoffs of 4 and 1, and the horizontal arrows indicate von Kluge's incentive to

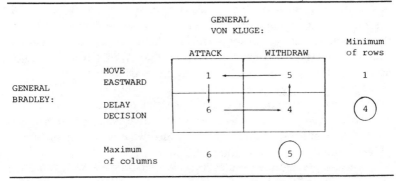

Figure 2.3 Reduced Outcome Matrix for the Battle of Avranches-Gap

move from the outcomes with payoffs of 5 and 6. Remember, the higher the payoff, the worse the outcomes for von Kluge.) Since there is no equilibrium outcome, the Battle of Avranches-Gap was not strictly determined. And from the Perfect Information Theorem, because this game lacks a saddlepoint, it is also not a game of perfect information.

In zero-sum games without a saddlepoint, then, there seems to be no resolution of the "he thinks, I think, he thinks" regress. Moreover, it appears that the principle that players in such a game should choose the strategy that maximizes their security level does not lead to an equilibrium outcome. Thus, the question of what strategy a player should choose remains unanswered.

One strategic principle does emerge, however, from an analysis of this game. Recall that in a game with a saddlepoint, a player is not hurt if the opponent knows in advance that the other player intends to select his or her optimal (i.e., equilibrium) strategy, though a player may be hurt if the opponent is able to determine that he or she intends to select a nonoptimal strategy. But in games without a saddlepoint, a player is *always* hurt, and the opponent is *always* helped, if that player's strategy choice is known in advance.

For example, without knowledge of von Kluge's strategy choice, Bradley could ensure a payoff of 4 (by selecting his delay strategy). But if he knew von Kluge's strategy choice, Bradley could guarantee a payoff of at least 5. Similarly, von Kluge could also ensure a payoff higher than that associated with his security level if he knew Bradley's strategy choice beforehand.

If a player is always hurt in a game without a saddlepoint when his opponent is able to determine his strategy choice, it follows that a player in such a game should attempt to keep this information from his opponent. Such an objective, however, could not be achieved if a player has a predetermined policy for selecting a strategy. Any patterned system, no matter how sophisticated or complex, is capable of being discovered. This suggests that players in a game without a saddlepoint should select their strategies at random, that is, mix their strategies according to some probability distribution over their set of pure strategies. A strategy generated at random according to a particular probability distribution is called a *mixed* strategy. Because it is random and, hence, cannot be predicted, the use of a mixed strategy can prevent one's opponent from discovering, in advance, what must ultimately be a player's choice of one or another pure strategy.

For a row player, like Bradley, in a two-person game with two pure strategies, a mixed strategy would take the form of the command "Select row 1 with probability p_1 and select row 2 with probability p_2," where $p_1 \geq 0$, $p_2 \geq 0$ and $p_1 + p_2 = 1$. Similarly, for a column player, like von Kluge, a mixed strategy would be the command "Select column 1 with probability q_1 and select column 2 with probability q_2," where $q_1 \geq 0$, $q_2 \geq 0$ and $q_1 + q_2 = 1$. A pure strategy, therefore, is a special case of a mixed strategy where the probability distribution by which a player selects a strategy assigns a probability of 1 to one pure strategy and a probability of 0 to all the player's remaining pure strategies.

If one accepts the proposition that players in a game without a saddlepoint should use a probability distribution to select a strategy, then the question that immediately arises is whether a best, or optimal, method exists for choosing a mixed strategy. Not surprisingly, the answer to this question is "yes."

The determination of an optimal mixed strategy rests upon the assumption that players should attempt to maximize their average or *expected payoffs*. An expected payoff is determined by summing the product of the payoff associated with each outcome and the probability that that outcome will occur. For example, if Bradley were to move eastward with probability p_1 and delay with probability p_2, and if von Kluge were to attack with probability q_1 and withdraw with probability q_2, then Bradley's expected payoff is given by the following expression:[9]

$$E(\text{Bradley}) = 1(p_1 q_1) + 5(p_1 q_2) + 6(p_2 q_1) + 4(p_2 q_2)$$

Since $p_1 + p_2 = 1$ and $q_1 + q_2 = 1$, $p_2 = (1 - p_1)$ and $q_2 = (1 - q_1)$. By substitution,

$$E(\text{Bradley}) = 1(p_1 q_1) + 5(p_1)(1 - q_1) + 6(1 - p_1)(q_1) + 4(1 - p_1)(1 - q_1)$$

And by multiplying through, and then summarizing,

$$E(\text{Bradley}) = -6(p_1 q_1) + p_1 + 2(q_1) + 4$$

To determine the values of p_1 and p_2 that maximize Bradley's expected payoff, a four-step manipulation process can be used.[10]

(1) First, factor out p_1 from the terms that include it, which gives
$$E(Bradley) = p_1(-6q_1 + 1) + 2(q_1) + 4$$

(2) Then, arrange the q_1 terms to have a coefficient of 1. Hence,
$$E(Bradley) = -6(p_1)(q_1 - \tfrac{1}{6}) + 2(q_1) + 4$$

(3) Next, by adding or subtracting a constant, arrange the second q_1 term to be the same as the first:
$$E(Bradley) = -6(p_1)(q_1 - \tfrac{1}{6}) + 2(q_1 - \tfrac{1}{6}) + 4 + (2)(\tfrac{1}{6})$$

(4) Finally, factor the q terms to manipulate the expression into the form $k(p_1 - a)(q_1 - b) + c$:
$$E(Bradley) = -6(p_1 - \tfrac{1}{3})(q_1 - \tfrac{1}{6}) + 4\tfrac{1}{3}$$

With the expression in this form, it can be seen that Bradley can ensure an expected payoff of $4\tfrac{1}{3}$ if he chooses to move eastward with probability $p_1 = \tfrac{1}{3}$ (and hence, chooses to delay with probability $p_2 = \tfrac{2}{3}$), no matter what strategy (q_1,q_2) von Kluge uses, since the first part of the expression is equal to zero and, hence, drops out when $p_1 = \tfrac{1}{3}$. Similarly, von Kluge, whose expected payoff is the negative of Bradley's, can ensure an expected payoff of $(-4\tfrac{1}{3})$ if he chooses to attack with probability $q_1 = \tfrac{1}{6}$, and, hence, to withdraw with probability $q_2 = \tfrac{5}{6}$.

It can be shown that the strategies $(\tfrac{1}{3}, \tfrac{2}{3})$ for Bradley and $(\tfrac{1}{6}, \tfrac{5}{6})$ for von Kluge are the optimal mixed strategies in this game. Their use has the effect of raising the security level for each player. (Recall that Bradley could ensure a payoff of 4, while von Kluge could ensure a payoff of −5, if each were limited to the selection of a single pure strategy.) In addition, the use of these strategies ensures for each player the value of the game, which, as in games with a saddlepoint, is the payoff that the row player (here, Bradley) can guarantee himself by selecting an optimal strategy (i.e., $4\tfrac{1}{3}$).

Since Bradley's optimal mixed strategy maximizes his minimum gain, it is called a maximin strategy. For similar reasons, von Kluge's optimal mixed strategy is called a minimax strategy. (Notice that these terms have not been applied to the *pure* strategy that appeared to maximize each player's security level in games without a saddlepoint.) Thus, in both categories of zero-sum games, the strategy that maximizes each player's security level is referred to as either a maximin or a minimax strategy.

Significantly, in games without a saddlepoint, optimal mixed strategies are in equilibrium. Neither player can increase the expected payoff by switching to another strategy if the opponent does not switch to a nonoptimal strategy.[11] In these games, then, just as in games with a saddlepoint, players are not helped, nor are their opponents hurt, if they know in advance that their opponents are going to choose their optimal strategy. Of course, a player always benefits in these games if he or she can determine the strategy the opponent will select on any one play of the game. Optimal mixed strategies have the advantage that they prevent one's opponent from obtaining this information.

In this context, it is worth noting the essential compatibility of equilibrium strategies in the two categories of zero-sum games. In games with a saddlepoint, players maximize their security level by choosing an optimal pure strategy, while they maximize their security level in games without a saddlepoint by choosing an optimal mixed strategy.

The similar characteristics of equilibrium strategies in two-person, finite, zero-sum games are summarized in the Fundamental Theorem of Game Theory, also called the Minimax Theorem.

> There exists a number v (the value of the game), a pure or mixed strategy (maximin strategy) for the row player which guarantees him at least v, and a pure or mixed strategy (minimax strategy) for the column player that guarantees that the row player gets at most v. These strategies are in equilibrium, and any pair of strategies in equilibrium yield a maximin and minimax strategy for the row and column player, respectively [Luce and Raiffa, 1957: 71].

Long thought unprovable until von Neumann did it in 1928, the Minimax Theorem provides a nice, neat solution for all finite, two-person zero-sum games by guaranteeing the existence of either a pure or mixed strategy equilibrium. Because these equilibrium strategies possess several attractive characteristics (discussed above) most game theorists consider them optimal and argue that rational players in zero-sum games should select them.

There are, however, some analysts who are less than sanguine about the solution specified by the Minimax Theorem. Though not in any way disparaging the aesthetic value of von Neumann's famous finding, they point out that there are several problems associated with interpreting the prescription that players in games without a saddlepoint should use a mixed strategy. It is to a discussion of some of these problems that we will now turn.

Some Problems with Mixed Strategies

One problem that immediately arises concerning the notion of a mixed strategy is its relevance in a game played only once. This difficulty stems from the fact that the concept of an expected payoff, the quantity that a rational player is assumed to desire to maximize, seems to apply only to a game repeated several times. But in a one-shot game, a player must ultimately choose a single pure strategy. Does a pure strategy selected according to a random probability distribution have meaning in such a context?

Critics say "no," and point out that even in repeated game situations there is a conflict between the prescription that players should choose an optimal mixed strategy and that players should attempt to maximize their security level. For example, suppose that the Avranches-Gap game is viewed as one of a series of battles in which similar strategy choices confront the generals on both sides. Also suppose that the random device—consistent with his optimal mixed strategy—that von Kluge used to select his strategy in this one battle indicates that he should choose his attack strategy, which at this point has an actual security level of –6. Since von Kluge's other (withdraw) strategy has a security level of –5, there seems to be a conflict between the two strategic principles, once an actual strategy is chosen.

The conflict between these two prescriptions may possibly shed some light on the strategies actually selected by the participants in this game. Consistent with the American military doctrine that a commander should base his decision on his opponent's capabilities rather than his intentions, Bradley delayed his decision, thereby selecting the pure strategy that maximized his security level. General von Kluge did likewise, and decided to withdraw, but his decision was countermanded by Hitler who ordered him to attack. Consequently, the battle Bradley most preferred to fight ensued. On the first day the gap held without reinforcement. On the second day Bradley ordered his four reserve divisions eastward, and they proceeded to surround most of the German Ninth Army, only remnants of which were able to escape.

If, for the sake of argument, one accepts the contention that Hitler's decision was a manifestation of a German mixed strategy, does the disastrous defeat of the Germans (after which von Kluge committed suicide) stand as a fatal indictment of this prescription? Defenders respond that in spite of occasional and statistically predictable setbacks, long-term or average payoffs are maximized when optimal mixed strategies are used. Moreover, even in a one-shot game, the use of a randomized procedure for selecting a strategy enables a player to keep from his opponent potentially damaging information about his planned strategy choice.

This response, however, ignores the fact that the calculation of an optimal mixed strategy, especially in games in which both players have more than two strategies, is not completely costless. Time, energy, and perhaps money must be expended to determine an optimal mixed strategy. Hence, in low-stakes games, players may prefer to use a nonoptimal strategy rather than incur the costs of determining an optimal strategy. In these games the normative arguments for using an optimal mixed strategy appear to be weak.

On the other hand, this criticism would not seem to apply to many high-stakes economic or political games. From a descriptive point of view, then, it seems reasonable to hypothesize that the strategies of players in games without a saddlepoint would tend to approximate their optimal level as the payoffs become larger.

This hypothesis, however, may not be easy to test, which raises still another difficulty with the concept of an optimal mixed strategy. In many empirical settings, it may be impossible to apply the axiomatically based procedure developed by von Neumann and Morgenstern (1953) or other methodologies for measuring cardinal utility (see, for example, Bueno de Mesquita, 1981). To the extent that this quantity is unmeasurable, the prescriptive or descriptive power of models that make use of the concept of an optimal mixed strategy is circumscribed.[12]

Concluding Comments

In summary, the conceptual neatness of two-person, zero-sum theory is marred somewhat by limitations associated with the concept of a mixed strategy. As will be seen, however, many of these problems evaporate in the theory of nonzero-sum games since the concept of a mixed strategy is of dubious relevance in other than a zero-sum context (Shubik, 1982: 249-251). Nonetheless, while some old problems become less relevant, new difficulties arise in the analysis of nonzero-sum games. These concerns will be delineated in the next chapter.

3. NONZERO-SUM GAMES:
THE REST OF THE CONTINUUM

Introduction

In Chapter 2, games of total conflict—that is, zero-sum games—were examined. In zero-sum games the interests of the players are diametrically opposed to one another. What one player wins, the other loses, and vice versa.

Conflict, however, need not be total; indeed, it rarely is. In most social, political or economic interactions, players generally have both competitive and complementary interests. Games of this sort are termed *nonzero-sum games, nonstrictly competitive games,* or *mixed-motive games.*

A Comparison of Zero-Sum and Nonzero-Sum Games

The structural characteristics of nonzero-sum games differ significantly from those of zero-sum games. To highlight these differences, consider now a nonzero-sum game played over three thousand years ago just outside of Troy. As Homer described the situation in *The Iliad* (cited in Schelling, 1966: 117), two warriors, Menelaos and Antilochos, were racing their chariots along a track that suddenly narrowed:

> Menelaos was driving in the middle of the road, hoping that no one would try to pass too close to his wheel, but Antilochos turned his horses out of the track and followed him a little to one side. This frightened Menelaos, and he shouted at him:
> "What reckless driving, Antilochos! Hold in your horses. This place is narrow, soon you will have more room to pass. You will foul my car and destroy us both!"

At this instant, Menelaos and Antilochos each had two strategies, either to cooperate (C) with the other by holding his horses, or to defect (D) from cooperation by driving his horses. In light of the competitive conditions under which this particular game was played, it seems safe to assume that the best outcome for each player was to win the race by driving his horses while the other held his, and that the worst outcome for both players was to terminate the race, and perhaps their lives—the noncooperative outcome, DD—by both driving their horses. In between, it is assumed that each player's next-best outcome, the cooperative or compromise outcome, CC, was a tie. This outcome would occur if both held their horses. Finally, each player's next-worst outcome was to lose the race, but not his life, by holding his horses when his opponent drove his.

These assumptions are reflected in the outcome matrix of Figure 3.1. In this matrix the best outcome of each player is represented by "4," the next-best outcome by "3," and so on. Recall from Chapter 1 that in nonzero-sum games two entries are required to represent the payoffs to

	MENELAOS:	
	HOLD HORSES (C)	DRIVE HORSES (D)
HOLD HORSES (C)	Compromise; race continues. (3,3)	Victory for Menelaos. (2,4)
DRIVE HORSES (D)	Victory for Antilochos. (4,2)	Possible collision. (1,1)

ANTILOCHOS:

Figure 3.1 Outcome Matrix for Racing Game (Chicken)

the players and that, by convention, the first entry in each cell of the matrix represents the payoff to the row player (here, Antilochos), while the second entry represents the payoff to the column player (here, Menelaos). Thus, (4,2) is the best outcome for Antilochos and the next-worst for Menelaos.

The racing game played by the two Greeks, defined by the structure of their preferences over the outcomes, is a specific example of a generic game called "Chicken." Chicken, which takes its name from a sadistic sport popular with some drivers in the 1950s, has received considerable attention from social scientists who have discerned in this game "a universal form of adversary engagement . . . not just a game played by delinquent teenagers with their hot-rods" (Schelling, 1966: 116).

Several salient differences between nonzero-sum games and zero-sum games are manifest in the Chicken game of Figure 3.1. These differences can readily be observed by considering the following four properties, true of all zero-sum games, but not generally true in nonzero-sum games.

1. In zero-sum games, players are unable to benefit by communicating prior to the game and deciding on a joint plan of action. Since the interests of the players are in total conflict, there is no room for cooperation through coordination. By contrast, in nonzero-sum games, players may benefit from collaboration. In this game of Chicken, for example, if Menelaos and Antilochos could have coordinated their strategies before the game began, they could have arranged to avoid the possibility of inducing their mutually worst outcome, (1,1), and perhaps, even have settled on their mutually advantageous outcome, (3,3).

2. In zero-sum games, players never benefit, and are sometimes hurt, by informing their opponents of their strategy choice prior to the play of a game. However, in nonzero-sum games, players may gain by announcing their strategy beforehand and making an "irrevocable commitment" to it. For example, in Chicken either player can ensure his or her best outcome by committing to the choice of his or her (D) strategy. In this case, the opponent, being rational, would have little choice but to "chicken out" and choose his or her (C) strategy. In effect, Antilochos used this tactic to win his race with Menelaos, though as Homer pointed out, "by trick, not by merit." After Menelaos shouted at him and urged him to hold his horses, "Antilochos only plied the whip and drove faster than ever, as if he did not hear." Eventually, Menelaos "fell behind: he let the horses go slow himself, for he was afraid that they might all collide in that narrow space" (cited in Schelling, 1966: 117).

3. In zero-sum games with more than one saddlepoint, equilibrium outcomes are equivalent—that is, yield the same payoff to each player—and interchangeable—that is, are found at the intersection of all equilibrium strategies. In nonzero-sum games, by contrast, equilibrium outcomes may be neither equivalent nor interchangeable. In Chicken, for example, there are two equilibrium outcomes, (4,2) and (2,4). Since they yield different payoffs for each player, they are not equivalent. Nor are they interchangeable. If, for instance, each player selects the strategy associated with the equilibrium outcome he or she preferred most, the resulting outcome would be (1,1), which is not an equilibrium outcome.

4. In zero-sum games, maximin and minimax strategies are equilibrium strategies, and vice versa. However, in nonzero-sum games this may not be the case. For instance, in Chicken, each player maximizes his or her security level by cooperating, and if both players cooperate, the compromise outcome (3,3) results. Yet this outcome is not stable. Hence, in nonzero-sum games maximin strategies do not necessarily lead to an equilibrium outcome. Nor are equilibrium strategies in nonzero-sum games necessarily maximin strategies. In Chicken, for example, each player's (D) strategy is associated with an equilibrium outcome. But, as just indicated, each player maximizes his or her security level by cooperating (C), not by defecting (D).

Of these differences between nonzero-sum and zero-sum games, the fact that equilibrium outcomes in nonzero-sum games may be neither equivalent nor interchangeable is the most significant. This characteristic of nonzero-sum games means that these games may have two or more equally attractive equilibrium outcomes, each possessing equivalent status as a solution, with no compelling reason to choose among them, and no guarantee that nonequilibria will not result when players choose strategies associated with an equilibrium outcome. Thus, despite the fact that all finite, nonzero-sum games have at least one equilibrium outcome in either pure or mixed strategies (Nash, 1951), the notion of an equilibrium outcome fails as a general solution concept for these games, and much of the mathematical neatness of zero-sum games evaporates when motives become mixed and conflict ceases to be total.

One should not be overly disappointed by this development since zero-sum games represent a degenerate case along the continuum of conflict. The assumption of diametrically opposed interests in these games vastly simplifies the real world, in which conflict and interdependency take on various guises. And although the general solution provided this class of games by the Minimax Theorem is theoretically elegant, it is limited, by its assumptions, in its empirical applicability.

On the other hand, nonzero-sum games more accurately represent the complexity of the real world. Thus it should not be surprising that game theorists are less than unified in their prescriptions for these games, or that a number of competing solution concepts, based upon distinctions that can sometimes be made between different equilibrium outcomes, exist in the literature.[13] Nevertheless, this should not be interpreted as a "deficiency" of *normative* game theory. As Bacharach (1977: 5-6) has argued, "the failure of game theory to give unambiguous solutions in certain classes of games does not necessarily imply that the theory is flawed, or inadequately developed. It may be in the nature of things."

The possible existence of two or more nonequivalent or noninterchangeable equilibrium outcomes does, however, present a potential stumbling block for the *descriptive* use of game theory in nonzero-sum situations, namely the problem of justifying the selection of one outcome in games in which multiple equilibria exist. If no criterion can be found for the selection of one outcome as the most likely societal state, the descriptive power of game-theoretic models for analyzing nonzero-sum conflicts is severely limited. For instance, although the primitive model of Figure 3.1 parsimoniously summarizes the problems inherent in the decision facing both Menelaos and Antilochos, it leaves unanswered what is perhaps the key question associated with their contest: Why did Antilochos, rather than Menelaos, win this particular race? Consequently, unless the set of equilibrium outcomes is narrowed considerably, very little can be said about how or why some conflicts are resolved, and very little insight is gained into the nature of some conflict interaction.

The other side of this coin, of course, is the lack of any equilibrium in many game situations. As was seen in Chapter 2, the analysis of zero-sum games, especially those played only once, is complicated when saddlepoints do not exist. Similar complexities occur in nonzero-sum games.[14]

One method for overcoming the difficulties associated with both of these problems—that is, for eliminating competing equilibria when multiple equilibria exist or for generating new equilibria when they do not—is to augment the concept of a rational decision by making stronger assumptions or adding institutional detail into the game analysis. Several techniques for supplementing unadorned game models will be illustrated in the remainder of this essay. While these methods do not always succeed in overcoming all of the problems associated with the concept of an equilibrium outcome, it should also be kept in mind that in many conflict situations, basic, unembellished game models do provide a useful and satisfying explanation of human behavior. For example, consider again Figure 1.4, which depicts the nonzero-sum game played by American and Israeli decision makers just prior to the outbreak of the 1967 Middle East war. Although there are two equilibria in this game—the two (4,3) outcomes—they are both equivalent and interchangeable. Since both are associated with Israel's strategy of resisting Nasser's decision to close the Strait of Tiran and with the American strategy of backing Israel, the notion of an equilibrium outcome is more than adequate to predict (or more accurately, retrodict) and explain the decisions and the eventual outcome in this game. Note, though, that the equilibrium associated with the tit-for-tat strategy of the United States provides a stronger explanation, since tit-for-tat dominates the D regardless strategy of the United States.

In the next several sections, some simple models will be used in a similar way to analyze a variety of conflict of interest situations. But before presenting these examples, and proceeding to a discussion of how game-theoretic models can be adapted to analyze more complex interactive situations, a more formal definition of Chicken will be given in order to facilitate a comparison with other games encountered in this chapter. To this end, consider Figure 3.2, which represents symbolically the strategies and outcomes of a 2 × 2 ordinal game. The letters representing the strategies and outcomes are mnemonic devices proposed by Rapoport and Chammah (1970). The meaning attached to the strategies, (C) for cooperation, (D) for defection, have already been noted. Rapoport and Chammah give the following interpretation to the payoffs: R stands for the reward of mutual cooperation, T for the

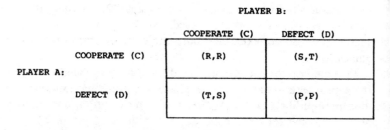

Figure 3.2   Symbolic Representation of a 2 × 2 Game

temptation to defect from that outcome, P for the punishment of mutual defection, and S for the sucker's payoff to the player who cooperates when the other does not. Chicken is defined by the order of each player's preferences over the set of outcomes, not the actual numerical values chosen arbitrarily in Figure 3.1. A game is Chicken when, for both players, $T > R > S > P$.

An Economic Policy Game[15]

One situation for which a game-theoretic framework illuminates the choices ultimately made by the players and, incidentally, illustrates President Reagan's skill as a strategist, occurred in the spring of 1981. At issue in this game, played between the Republican and Democratic leaders in the House and Senate, was the implementation of the president's economic program for the upcoming fiscal year. As Leonard Silk described this game in two columns in the *New York Times* (April 10 and 15, 1981), the Democrats had two strategies: (1) to mainly support the Reagan program, or (2) to attack the program and present their own plan. In turn, the Republicans had to decide whether to defend the president's program or reach a compromise on budget issues with the Democrats, who were in the majority in the House. The outcomes associated with each of these strategy choices, and Silk's estimates of each player's ordinal ranking of these outcomes, are depicted in Figure 3.3.

This game was played in the Senate first. Perhaps because the Democrats were in the minority, they offered little opposition to Reagan's economic program, while the Republicans supported the President completely. The Democrats' next-worst outcome and the Republicans' best outcome (2,4) was thereby reduced.

The story was somewhat different in the House. There, the Democrats attacked the Reagan package and introduced a "counterbudget."

		REPUBLICANS:	
		SUPPORT REAGAN COMPLETELY	COMPROMISE
DEMOCRATS:	MAINLY SUPPORT REAGAN	Republicans win; Democrats avoid blame. (2,4)	Republicans win but vex Reagan; Democrats share credit. (3,3)
	ATTACK REAGAN	Republican program blocked in House; Democrats incur blame. (1,2)	Republicans lose much of program; Democrats look fiscally responsible. (4,1)

SOURCE: Leonard Silk's Economic Scene, "Game Theory: Reagan's Move," New York Times, April 15, 1981, p. D2. Copyright ©1981 by The New York Times Company. Reprinted by permission.

Figure 3.3 A 1981 Economic Policy Game

The Republicans continued to support the president and consequently induced the worst outcome for the Democrats and the next-worst outcome for the Republicans (1,2).

Clearly, this outcome was unsatisfactory, for both sides. What should be done? Some presidential aides argued that the president ought to try to forge a compromise with the Democrats. Perhaps to marshal support for this recommendation, three sub-Cabinet officers had even led the chairman of the House Budget Committee to believe that the president would accept a compromise in the form of a one-year, rather than a three-year, tax cut. Such a compromise outcome (3,3) was better for both the Republicans and Democrats than the deadlock (1,2) outcome they found themselves in. Columnist Silk agreed with this prescription. He opined that the compromise was "actually the best outcome for both parties under the circumstances."

The problem with the compromise outcome, however, was that it was not stable. If the Republicans publicly offered to compromise, the Democrats could induce their best outcome and the Republicans worst outcome (4,1) by maintaining their attack on the Republicans' economic agenda. Moreover, from the Republican point of view, their compromise strategy was dominated by their support strategy. Not surprisingly then, the president rejected the advice of his aides and ordered his staff to repudiate a report that he was willing to compromise. Put another way, the President was sticking to his dominant strategy; eventually, House Democrats were forced to support his program. The unique equilibrium outcome in this game (2,4), and the rational outcome for both parties, was subsequently induced, perhaps proving, as Silk later argued, that the president was "a natural and gifted game theorist."

A Watergate Game

In the preceding example, President Reagan apparently proved himself to be a better strategist than his staff and opposition. Sometimes, however, the most proficient strategists are not the actual players in a game, but rather are those who design or manipulate games that others play. This was the case with Assistant U.S. Attorney Earl Silbert who, by means of a simple but brilliant ploy, was able to induce the cooperation of John Dean in the investigation of the so-called Watergate affair.

As Muzzio (1982) described the background to this game, shortly after the arrest of seven men for breaking into the headquarters of the Democratic National Committee in the Watergate complex on June 17, 1972, a multilevel conspiracy formed to conceal White House complicity in the break-in. The lowest level of this conspiracy was composed of the Watergate burglars, including G. Gordon Liddy, counsel to the Committee to Reelect the President, and James McCord, the committee's security chief. The key figure of the midlevel conspiracy group was John Dean, counsel to the president. Of course, the highest level included the president and his closest advisers.

In cases involving multiple defendants, especially in conspiracy cases like this one, a common strategy of prosecuting attorneys is to try to induce one of the conspirators to testify against his or her compatriots by offering a recommendation for leniency at the time of sentencing.[16] Multilevel or hierarchical conspiracy cases like Watergate are usually broken by "dealing up." Once the low-level defendants are implicated, they may be granted immunity to induce them to testify against those at the next level.

Although successful at first, the lowest level of this conspiracy began to break when McCord, faced with the prospect of a lengthy prison sentence, decided to cooperate with the prosecution. McCord's defection alone, however, was insufficient to link the bottom to the midlevel of conspirators since McCord had no first-hand information of the participation of higher-ups in the planning of the break-in. What McCord knew came from Liddy, who was the key link between the two levels. Unless Liddy broke, the White House containment strategy would be successful; only the lowest level men would be implicated, and

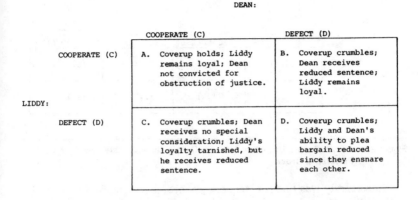

Figure 3.4 Outcome Matrix for the Dean-Liddy Game

Silbert, who was convinced that more important figures were involved, would be unable to prove his supposition and crack his case.

In a way, then, Liddy was involved in a game with each of the midlevel conspirators. For example, consider the situation as Dean probably interpreted it in March 1973. In this game both he and Liddy had two options: They could either continue to cooperate in the conspiracy (C), or defect (D) and cooperate with the prosecution. Depending upon what strategy each selected, one of four outcomes, summarized in Figure 3.4, could result.

The rationale behind the "Silbert ploy" can be appreciated by comparing the decision that Dean would have made in this game had he been aware of Liddy's true preferences with the putative game, devised by Silbert, that he thought he was playing. As we now know, Liddy, with a very strong (and perhaps misguided) sense of loyalty, preferred to cooperate with the other conspirators no matter what they did. In game-theoretic terms, this means that his (C) strategy dominated his (D) strategy. Thus it seems safe to assume that Liddy's preference order was (A,B,C,D).[17]

In contrast to Liddy's preferences, Dean's were more conventional. As Muzzio points out, although Dean most preferred that the conspiracy hold (A), he naturally preferred a reduced sentence (B) to the sentence he would receive with no special consideration shown (D), and (D) to having the book thrown at him (C). Dean's preference order, therefore, was (A,B,D,C).

		DEAN:			
		C REGARDLESS	D REGARDLESS	TIT-FOR-TAT (C/D)	TAT-FOR-TIT (D/C)
LIDDY:	C	(4,4)	(3,3)	(4,4)	(3,3)
	D	(2,1)	(1,2)	(1,2)	(2,1)

Figure 3.5   Initial Dean-Liddy Game, Given Dean's Correct Assessment of Liddy's Preference Order

Since Liddy was under arrest and, hence, made the first choice, the game that Dean would have played with Liddy, if Liddy's true preferences were known, is properly depicted as a 2 × 4 game (see Figure 3.5). In this game Liddy had two strategies, while Dean had four, each contingent on Liddy's two strategy choices.

If this game were actually played—and it was until Silbert's ploy—Liddy's (C) strategy would remain dominant. Dean also had a dominant strategy, tit-for-tat, which implied his cooperation given his preception of Liddy's dominant (C) strategy. Thus, even after McCord agreed to cooperate with the prosecution, Dean and other midlevel conspirators had no incentive to do likewise, and would continue to have no incentive as long as they perceived Liddy's (C) strategy to be dominant. In this case the conspiracy would hold, and the prosecution would remain frustrated.

It was at this point that Silbert, facing the prospect of failure, devised his ingenious maneuver. On March 26, after reconvening the grand jury, the prosecutors got orders granting each of the low-level conspirators immunity from further prosecution in return for their testimony. Liddy, who still refused to talk, was kept in an anteroom for several hours by the prosecution who hoped to make it appear that he was turning state's evidence. To further this illusion, they even asked Liddy's attorney to tell the press that Liddy was cooperating. Liddy's attorney, however, refused. Instead, as Silbert had hoped, he told reporters, in a rather strong protest, that his client would continue to remain silent. Perhaps concluding that Liddy's attorney was protesting too much, Dean contacted his attorney that same afternoon and began talking "off the record" with the prosecution.

In his first meeting with Dean on April 8, Silbert reinforced his lie by telling him that "Liddy's been talking to us privately." In game-theoretic

		DEAN:			
		C REGARDLESS	D REGARDLESS	TIT-FOR TAT (C/D)	TAT-FOR TIT (D/C)
LIDDY:	C	(2,4)	(1,3)	(2,4)	(1,3)
	D	(4,1)	(3,2)	(3,2)	(4,1)

Figure 3.6 Liddy-Dean Game, Given Dean's Incorrect Assessment of Liddy's Preference Order

terms, Silbert was trying to convince Dean that Liddy's (C) strategy was no longer dominant. If this were the case, Liddy's preference scale must be (C,D,A,B) (Muzzio, 1982: 46-47).

Dean, of course, believed Silbert's misrepresentation, and consequently thought he was playing the game depicted in Figure 3.6. In this game, Liddy's (D) strategy appears dominant to Dean, while Dean's tit-for-tat strategy remains dominant. But in this case Dean's dominant strategy implied that he defect from the conspiracy and cooperate with the prosecution. He did! The Silbert plot worked; i.e., the prosecutors had succeeded in dealing up. Soon they would reach the top.

A Biblical Game

In an ingenious application, Brams (1980) uses simple game-theoretic models to offer an exegesis of several stories, such as that of Abraham's attempted sacrifice of his son, Isaac, from the Old Testament. In examining this game, Brams asks whether a faith or a rationality interpretation, or both, sustains Abraham's decision to sacrifice Isaac.

Brams begins by positing a game between God and Abraham. Abraham's choices are simple: either to obey God and offer Isaac (0), or to disobey God and not offer Isaac ($\overline{0}$). God, in turn, could either (1) cooperate by reneging (if Isaac were offered) or relenting (if not), (R), or (2) not cooperate by not reneging (if Isaac were offered) or not relenting (if not), ($\overline{R}$). The consequences of the strategy choices of God and Abraham are summarized in Figure 3.7.

In this game, God's preferences are straightforward. Given His subsequent decision to spare Isaac, it seems safe to assume that He preferred that Abraham show his faith by offering Isaac, and given that Isaac is offered, that He preferred to renege and not demand that Isaac be sacrificed. On the other hand, if Isaac were not offered, Brams assumed that God would prefer to press the issue, and not relent.

God

		Renege (if Isaac offered)/ relent (if not): R	Don't renege/relent: R̄
Abraham	Offer Isaac: O	Abraham faithful, God merciful, Isaac saved — a. (4,4) b. (4,4) c. (4,4)	Abraham faithful, God adamant, Isaac sacrificed — a. (3,3) b. (2,3) c. (1,3)
	Don't offer Isaac: Ō	Abraham resistant, God merciful, Isaac saved — a. (2,1) b. (3,1) c. (3,1)	Abraham resistant, God adamant, Isaac's fate uncertain — a. (1,2) b. (1,2) c. (2,2)

Key:

(x,y) = (Abraham, God)

4 = best; 3 = next best; 2 = next worst; 1 = worst

a. *Abraham faithful regardless:* prefers "offer" over "don't offer"

b. *Abraham wavers somewhat:* prefers God "renege/relent" over "don't renege/relent"

c. *Abraham wavers seriously:* Isaac's life paramount—same as (b) above except if God adamant, would prefer "don't offer"

SOURCE: S. J. Brams, **Biblical Games: A Strategic Analysis of Stories in the Old Testament**, Fig. 3.1, p. 39. Copyright © 1980 by The MIT Press. Reprinted by permission.

Figure 3.7 Outcome Matrix for Abraham's Sacrifice

In contrast to God's preferences, Abraham's motivations seem more problematic. Three equally reasonable assumptions might be made:

(a) *Abraham faithful regardless.* Under this interpretation, Abraham prefers to offer Isaac regardless of what God does subsequently.

(b) *Abraham wavers somewhat.* Under this interpretation, Abraham prefers that God relents regardless of what he does, although he still prefers to show his faith and offer Isaac provided God relents.

(c) *Abraham wavers seriously.* This interpretation is the same as (b), except here, given that God is not cooperative, Abraham prefers not to offer Isaac.

In Figure 3.7, three sets of preference orders, suggested by the different assumptions about Abraham's motives, are given. But since God and Abraham did not make their choices simultaneously, the game they played is properly represented by a 2 × 4 matrix with Abraham, who made the first choice, having two strategies and God, who made the second choice, having four. A 2 × 4 normal-form representation of each of the three possible interpretations of this game is provided in Figure 3.8.

For each of the matrices of Figure 3.8, God's R/R̄ (tit-for-tat) strategy is dominant. Interestingly, however, Abraham has a dominant strategy (i.e., to offer Isaac) only under assumption (a). Brams (1980: 43) argues that only the game implied by assumption (a) is consistent with a faith interpretation of Abraham's motives.

To obey God blindly is, in fact, to act *as if* one has a dominant strategy—an unconditionally best choice—that requires no detailed preference information about the other player, much less an anticipation of what strategy he might choose.

Because Abraham does not have a dominant strategy in either of the games implied by assumptions (b) and (c), these two games are not consistent with a faith interpretation of his motives. A sagacious Abraham in these two games must exhibit game-theoretic rationality, that is, he must take into account God's preferences and the strategy choices they imply if he wishes to maximize his utility.

In all three interpretations, however, Abraham induces the best outcome of both players, (4,4), by offering Isaac. This, of course, is the outcome the Bible tells us occurred. Thus, on "empirical grounds," a

a. *Abraham faithful regardless*: whatever God chooses subsequently—renege/relent (R) or not (R̄)—Abraham prefers to offer (O).

		God			God		
		R	R̄	R/R	R̄/R̄	R/R̄	R̄/R
Abraham	O	(4,4)	(3,3)	(4,4)	(3,3)	(4,4)	(3,3)	← Offer dominant
	Ō	(2,1)	(1,2)	(2,1)	(1,2)	(1,2)	(2,1)	

(4,4) in R/R̄ column circled.

↑
Tit-for-tat dominant

b. *Abraham wavers somewhat*: whatever Abraham chooses—offer (O) or don't offer (Ō)—he prefers God subsequently renege/relent (R).

		God			God		
		R	R̄	R/R	R̄/R̄	R/R̄	R̄/R
Abraham	O	(4,4)	(2,3)	(4,4)	(2,3)	(4,4)	(2,3)
	Ō	(3,1)	(1,2)	(3,1)	(1,2)	(1,2)	(3,1)

(4,4) in R/R̄ column circled. } Neither strategy dominant—
must anticipate God's choice.

↑
Tit-for-tat dominant

c. *Abraham wavers seriously*: same as (b) above, except given God is adamant (R̄), Abraham prefers not to offer (Ō).

		God			God		
		R	R̄	R/R	R̄/R̄	R/R̄	R̄/R
Abraham	O	(4,4)	(1,3)	(4,4)	(1,3)	(4,4)	(1,3)
	Ō	(3,1)	(2,2)	(3,1)	(2,2)	(2,2)	(3,1)

(4,4) in R/R̄ column circled. } Neither strategy dominant—
must anticipate God's choice

↑
Tit-for-tat dominant

Key:
(x,y) = (Abraham, God)
4 = best; 3 = next best; 2 = next worst; 1 = worst
Circled outcome rational

Figure 3.8 Payoff Matrices for Abraham's Sacrifice

faith interpretation cannot be distinguished from a rationality interpretation of Abraham's actions. In other words, a rationality interpretation is as proficient in explaining Abraham's decision as is a faith interpretation.

It is also interesting to note that if God's intention in this game was to gauge Abraham's faith, He failed.

	SUSPECT B:	
	NOT CONFESS (C)	CONFESS (D)
SUSPECT A: NOT CONFESS (C)	(-1,-1)	(-10,0)
CONFESS (D)	(0,-10)	(-5,-5)

Figure 3.9 Prisoners' Dilemma

Although God's harrowing test of Abraham succeeds in establishing that Abraham will obey His command—however ghastly—Abraham may well have done so for reasons other than faith. Hence, God's test does not assuredly dispel doubts about Abraham's faith, given that Abraham knows God's preferences and is rational [Brams, 1980: 45].

Even a seriously wavering (and rational) Abraham passes this test.

Prisoners' Dilemma and the Problem of Inefficient Equilibria

In the preceding example, even though God may have failed to devise a test that was sensitive enough to measure Abraham's faith, He did quite well. Abraham did obey His command by offering his son, and God, by subsequently sparing Isaac, induced His, and Abraham's, best outcome.

Not all games, of course, have such happy endings. The game depicted in Figure 3.9 is an unfortunate case in point. This game, known as Prisoners' Dilemma,[18] takes its name from a story used to illustrate its structure. Two suspects are taken into custody. The district attorney is convinced that they are guilty of a certain crime but does not have enough evidence to convince a jury. Consequently, he separates the suspects and tells each one that he has two choices: to either confess (D) or not confess (C) to the crime. The suspects are told that if both confess, neither will receive special consideration and will therefore receive a jail sentence of five years. If neither confesses, both will probably be convicted of some minor charge and have to spend one year in jail. But if one confesses and the other does not, the suspect who confesses will be set free for cooperating with the state while the suspect that does not will have the book thrown at him and receive a ten-year sentence. (Notice the similarity between this story and the situation faced by John Dean.) What should each suspect do?

Notice from Figure 3.9 that confessing (D) dominates not confessing (C) for both players; that is, each does better by confessing than by not confessing, regardless of the strategy chosen by the other. For instance, if B confesses, A gets ten years in jail if he does not confess and only five years if he confesses. If B does not confess, A gets one year in jail by not confessing and is set free if he confesses. Since this game is symmetric, a similar logic characterizes B's choices.

Dominant strategies are unconditionally best strategies. Therefore, each suspect's optimal strategy is to confess. Observe that if *both* suspects use their optimal strategy and confess, both are worse off than if they both use their nonoptimal strategy and do not confess. If both confess, the outcome that results (-5,-5)—the unique equilibrium outcome in this game—is each suspect's next-worse outcome, but if both do not confess, each suspect obtains his next best outcome (-1, -1). Paradoxically, since each suspect has a dominant strategy, it remains true that each suspect is *individually* better off using it and confessing.

Technically, the unique equilibrium outcome in this game is said to be *non-Pareto-optimal* (or *Pareto-deficient*), that is, at least one player would do better and the other would do no worse by switching to another outcome. In this example, both players prefer (-1,-1) to (-5,-5). Conversely, the three non-equilibria are all *Pareto-optimal*, that is, each is preferred to any other outcome by *at least* one player. For instance, (-1,-1) is preferred to (0,-10) by B, to (-10,0) by A, and to (-5,-5) by both suspects.

Among the 78 distinct 2 × 2 games identified by Rapoport and Guyer (1966), Prisoners' Dilemma alone is characterized by these two features, i.e., dominant strategies leading to a Pareto-deficient equilibrium. Alternatively, this game can be defined by the rank order of the player's preferences over the set of outcomes. Referring back to the symbolic representation of a 2 × 2 game depicted in Figure 3.2, a game is defined as a Prisoners' Dilemma when, for both players, $T > R > P > S$. This ranking ensures that each player has a dominant strategy that results in a Pareto-deficient equilibrium outcome.[19]

Prisoners' Dilemma, game theory's most famous game, has spawned an enormous amount of theoretical and experimental research. There is a good reason for this. The conflict between individual and collective interest, highlighted and neatly summarized in this game, lies at the heart of many important real-life situations with implications for political, social, economic, and other kinds of systems. Many economists, for instance, hold the structure of this game responsible for phenomena such as price wars and trade barriers; and international relations specialists frequently associate the logic of arms races with that of a Prisoners' Dilemma game.

In such situations, then, players in a Prisoners' Dilemma game may, willy-nilly, find themselves caught in a "catch 22" situation in which they are done in by their rational calculations. Even though they are both better off if they cooperate, the irrefutable logic of a dominant strategy dictates that each player, in pursuing his own selfish ends, defect from cooperation. In many significant real world games, therefore, there may be "no invisible hand that brings the self-interest of one individual into harmony with the self-interest of another" (van den Doel, 1979: 55).

Clearly, the paradoxical nature of the individually rational but collectively irrational solution to this game has important ramifications for nations, in both their internal and external affairs. Internally, if, in certain kinds of situations, individual members of a society are doomed to frustrate themselves and produce nonoptimal outcomes, the case for increased governmental involvement in the private sector and cen-tralized economic and political control would appear to be very strong. Indeed, the primary justification given by some political philosophers for the very existence of the state is the premise that individuals in Prisoners' Dilemma-like situations will not cooperate with one another. Externally, if nations are unable to devise mechanisms for cooperating with each other in areas of fundamental importance, we are condemned to live in a world in which conflict is the norm and in which international peace is but a respite for states preparing themselves for the next round of a prize fight without a final bell, except perhaps in the case of apocalypse.

Paradox Lost?

Is the world subject to such a fate or can the logic of the Prisoners' Dilemma game be surmounted? In this section this question will be addressed and several proposed solutions to the dilemma of the prisoners examined.

Binding agreements and communication. The original story used to illustrate Prisoners' Dilemma assumed that the two suspects were unable to communicate and make a binding agreement. It is clear that if the prisoners are permitted to communicate *and* make a binding agreement, the dilemma disappears. They could simply negotiate a contract to cooperate. The dilemma dissolves if the enforcement provisions of the contract change the structure of each player's preferences over the set of outcomes. Presumably, penalties imposed for breaking the contract would make defection costly, so that for each player $R > T > P > S$.

But binding and enforceable agreements may not be available to players in many situations. For example, with no present overarching authority in the international system, international agreements—i.e., treaties—though theoretically binding, are not strictly enforceable (except perhaps by the sword) and are subject to abrogation when a state's national interest is at stake. Or two competing corporations, faced with a pricing decision, may be prohibited from explicitly colluding with each other by antitrust laws.[20]

Still, there are many situations in which there are no restrictions on player communication, even though binding agreements might be precluded. Perhaps through rational discourse and by recognizing each other's interests, players in a Prisoners' Dilemma game can agree to cooperate.

Although this is an intuitively appealing resolution, it is deficient. Even if the two suspects could communicate and negotiate an agreement, each would have an incentive to defect and break it. And if both defect, the noncooperative outcome DD results. In other words, as the game is formulated, the cooperative outcome CC cannot be considered a solution because it is not stable. This instability is as much a part of the dilemma as is the fact that each player's dominant strategy produces a Pareto-deficient outcome. Thus it must be concluded that preplay communication in itself does not dissipate the dilemma of the prisoners.

Sequencing. If binding agreements are not available, and if communication alone does not lead to a compromise outcome, perhaps other, ordinary features of the real world, abstracted away by game-theoretic models, will make cooperation rational in a Prisoners' Dilemma-type game. Snyder and Diesing (1977: 44) claim that this is the case if the standard game-theoretic assumption of simultaneous play is dropped and sequential strategy choice is assumed. If players select their strategies sequentially,

> there is no problem about guessing whether or not the opponent is trustworthy and whether to doublecross him if he is or to preempt if he isn't. This is because even if the opponent proves to be non-cooperative—plays his D strategy—there is time to counter with one's own D strategy, thus avoiding the disastrous CD or DC outcomes. Since both parties know that such countering is inevitable, neither has any incentive to play D and the logical

		SUSPECT B:			
		(C) REGARDLESS	(D) REGARDLESS	C/D TIT-FOR-TAT	D/C TAT-FOR-TIT
SUSPECT A:	(C)	(-1,-1)	(-10,0)	(-1,-1)	(-10,0)
	(D)	(0,-10)	(-5,-5)	(-5,-5)	(0,-10)

Figure 3.10 Outcome Matrix for a Sequentially Played Prisoners' Dilemma Game

outcome of the Prisoners' Dilemma with sequential moves is CC, mutual cooperation.

Does sequential play solve the Prisoners' Dilemma? To answer this question, consider the matrix representation of a sequentially played Prisoners' Dilemma game depicted in Figure 3.10. An examination of Figure 3.10 reveals that in the sequentially played version, Suspect A, assumed to choose first, no longer has a dominant strategy. His optimal strategy depends on the choice of B. But the choice of (D) remains dominant for B. Given B's dominant strategy, A maximizes his payoff by also choosing (D), which induces his next-worst outcome, rather than (C), which induces his worst outcome. The resulting outcome, DD, remains the unique equilibrium in this game, and the rationale for considering it the solution to the sequentially played variant of Prisoners' Dilemma is just as compelling as it is for the simultaneously played version. Consequently, sequential choice, like the ability of the players to communicate, does not alleviate the dilemma faced by the two suspects.

Nonmyopic rationality. Although sequential choice does not resolve the Prisoners' Dilemma, some very interesting results obtain if the process is taken just one step further. To see this, consider now the concept of a *nonmyopic equilibrium,*[21] developed by Brams and Wittman (1981). Underlying the concept of a nonmyopic equilibrium is the assumption that the following rules of play operates in 2 × 2 ordinal games:

(1) Both players simultaneously choose strategies, thereby defining an *initial outcome* of the game.
(2) Once at an initial outcome, either player can unilaterally switch strategies and change that outcome to a subsequent outcome.
(3) The other player can respond by unilaterally switching strategies, thereby moving the game to a new outcome.

(4) These strictly alternating moves continue until the player with the next move chooses not to switch strategies. When this happens, the game terminates, and the outcome reached is the *final outcome* (Brams and Hessel, 1982).

The concept of a nonmyopic equilibrium also assumes that players are able to anticipate the consequences of strategy choices made in games governed by these rules. Put another way, this equilibrium concept is a look-ahead idea that assumes that a player will evaluate the consequences of departing from an initial outcome, taking into account the probable response of the other player, his own counterresponse, subsequent counterresponses, and so on. If for *both* players the starting outcome is preferred to the outcome each player calculates he will end up at by making an initial departure, the starting outcome is a nonmyopic equilibrium.

Given these assumptions, it is easy to demonstrate that a strategy supporting the compromise outcome (-1,-1) in Prisoners' Dilemma is both stable and farsightedly rational. To see this, consider the game tree depicted in Figure 3.11, which lists the sequence of moves and countermoves implied by a departure of suspect A away from (-1,-1) in the Prisoners' Dilemma game of Figure 3.9. A's incentive to move from this outcome can be determined simply by working backwards up the tree and asking what the rational choice of each player is at each node or decision point. If the outcome implied by this process is inferior to (-1,-1) for A, then this outcome is stable in a nonmyopic sense for A. If a similar calculation also reveals that this outcome is stable in the nonmyopic sense for B, then this outcome is a nonmyopic equilibrium.

At the last node on the tree, B must choose between staying at (-10,0)—his best outcome—or moving to (-1,-1)—his next-best outcome. Clearly, should this node be reached in a sequence of moves and countermoves, B will rationally choose to stay.

But would such a sequence ever rationally get to this point? To determine this, consider A's choice at (-5,-5). At this node, A is faced with a choice of staying at (-5,-5)—his next-worst outcome—or moving to (-10,0)—his worst outcome. Given this choice, A would not switch strategies, thereby terminating the sequence of moves before B can choose at (-10,0).

Given A's rational choice at (-5,-5), what should B do at the preceding node? Here B can decide to stay at (0,-10)—his worst outcome—or move to (-5,-5)—his next-worst outcome which, because of the expected choice of A, would become the final outcome. For B, the rational choice is to move.

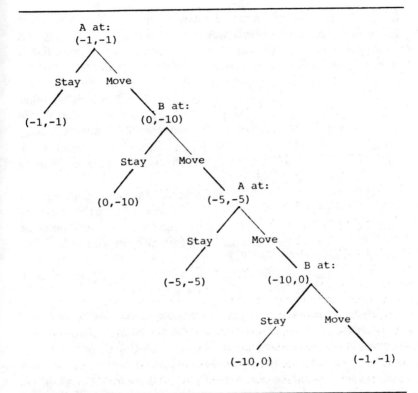

Figure 3.11 Game Tree Representation of Moves in Prisoners' Dilemma, Starting with Suspect A at (-1, -1)

What should A do at the previous node? A can either stay at (-1,-1)—his next-best outcome—or move to his best outcome at (0,-10). However, as was just seen, a move to (0,-10) implies (-5,-5) as a final outcome in a sequence of moves and countermoves. Since A prefers (-1,-1) to (-5,-5), he should stay at (-1,-1). And since A has no incentive to depart from (-1,-1), the cooperative outcome is a nonmyopic equilibrium for A.

It is also a nonmyopic equilibrium for B. By symmetry, the calculus facing B at (-1,-1) is the same as A's. And since neither player has an incentive to move away from (-1,-1), this outcome is a nonmyopic equilibrium.

The compromise outcome, however, is not the only nonmyopic equilibrium in Prisoners' Dilemma. The noncooperative outcome, (-5,-5)—the unique Nash equilibrium and the conventional solution to this game—is also stable in the nonmyopic sense. If this outcome is the initial outcome, neither player would have an incentive to change his strategy because the player with the subsequent move would immediately terminate the process at the outcome best for him and worst for the departing player—either $(0,-10)$ or $(-10,0)$.

More significant, though, is the fact that $(-5,-5)$ "absorbs" all other outcomes, including itself, except for $(-1,-1)$. This means that should either $(0,-10)$ or $(-10,0)$ be reached in a sequence of alternating strategy choices, the outcome that would be chosen would be $(-5,-5)$, not $(-1,-1)$. Thus, the very calculations that enhance the stability of the compromise outcome can also undermine it.

Nevertheless, the cooperative outcome remains a nonmyopic equilibrium in this game. It thus provides a solution of sorts to the Prisoners' Dilemma. Provided that the cooperative outcome is the initial outcome and that players can make and evaluate the consequences of an unlimited number of moves and countermoves,[22] a strategy supporting the compromise outcome in a Prisoners' Dilemma game is both farsightedly rational and stable over the long term.

Extended play. Admittedly, the conditions underlying the nonmyopic stability of the compromise outcome in Prisoners' Dilemma are somewhat restrictive and may not always be satisfied. Are there any other circumstances under which rational players might cooperate in such a game? Some theorists have argued that cooperation is rational when players are faced with repeated plays of this game with the same opponent. For instance, Luce and Raiffa (1957: 101) assert that they would not choose (D) at every move if this game were played more than once, but would try to teach the other player to cooperate by rewarding him if he does and punishing him if he does not. It is hoped that, if such a strategy is used,

> an unarticulated collusion between the two players will develop, much in the same way as a mature economic market often exhibits a marked degree of collusion without any communication among the participants.

And Davis (1983: 113) has suggested, though without proof, that Luce and Raiffa's argument has merit, but only when the number of times the game is repeated is not known.

Is this intuition justified? To answer this, assume the number of times the game will be repeated is not fixed.[23] Under these circumstances, it also seems reasonable to assume that the players will discount the value of their future payoffs, that is, that they value a present payoff more than a payoff received at some unspecified time in the future. This does not mean that future payoffs are seen as worthless, just worth less.[24]

Since the number of strategies available to each player in an iterated game is potentially very large, it may be unreasonable to assume that a player will survey, or even attempt to survey, all possible strategies available to him in a repeated game. According to Taylor (1976: 32-33), the following strategies are most likely to be considered by the players, at least on a conscious level:

D^∞: (D) is chosen every time the game is repeated.

C^∞: (C) is chosen every time the game is repeated.

A_k: (C) is chosen in the first game and in every subsequent game as long as the other player chooses (C). If the other player chooses (D), (D) is selected for the next k games regardless of what the other player does. Then (C) is chosen until the other player chooses (D), in which case (D) is chosen for the next k + 1 games and so on.

B: (C) is chosen in the first game, and the choice of the other player is chosen in the next and subsequent games.

B': Same as B except that (D) is chosen in the first game. (B and B' are two variations of a tit-for-tat strategy.)

Are any of the $5 \times 5 = 25$ outcomes resulting from these five strategies equilibria?

If one assumes that only these strategies are considered by the players, the outcome (D^∞, D^∞) will always be an equilibrium in the iterated game—or the *supergame,* as it is sometimes referred to—since a single player cannot do better by unilaterally switching to one of the four other strategies. Conversely, (C^∞, C^∞) is never an equilibrium since one player can always improve his payoff by switching to (D) for the remaining plays of the game. In addition, as Taylor (1976: 31-43) shows, depending on the rate at which the players discount future payoffs, and the value of the payoffs in the component games, the following are sometimes equilibria:

(1) The four pairs in which each player uses either A_k or B. In each case, the outcome is mutual cooperation in every ordinary game throughout the supergame.

(2) The three pairs in which each player chooses B' and the other player B' or D^∞. In each case, the outcome is mutual defection throughout the supergame.

(3) The two strategy pairs (B,B') and (B',B). Here, the outcome is an *alternation* throughout the supergame of (C,D) in one ordinary game and (D,C) in the next, beginning with (C,D) in the first game in the case of (B,B') and with (D,C) in the case of (B',B).

In an empirical sense, equilibria of category (3) do not seem relevant for many situations, such as arms races, involving repeated plays of a Prisoners' Dilemma game. Since minor complications are introduced when category (3) equilibria are admitted (Taylor, 1976: 88-89), they will be rejected on empirical grounds to facilitate the subsequent discussion. If category (3) equilibria are eliminated from consideration, then it is possible for some or all four of the mutual defection equilibria to coexist with some or all of the mutual cooperation equilibria of category (1). Basically, this occurs if each player's discounting of future payoffs is "sufficiently" low, that is, if each player does not prefer the payoff resulting from unilateral defection in the first component game and mutual defection in all subsequent component games to the payoff resulting from mutual cooperation throughout the repeated game (Taylor, 1976: 89). Since each mutual cooperation equilibrium is both equivalent and interchangeable with every other one, and in addition is Pareto-optimal under these conditions, it is clear that if at least one equilibrium of category (1) exists, the outcome of the iterated Prisoners' Dilemma game will result in the repeated selection of CC on every move of the game!

Before euphoria takes over, however, it is important to remember that this result applies only when the limited number of strategies considered by Taylor are available to the players. But, as two recent computer tournaments (Axelrod, 1980a, 1980b) demonstrate, these five strategies hardly exhaust the set of reasonable strategies. Hence the relevance of Taylor's results to a wide variety of empirical situations must remain suspect.

By contrast, Axelrod's (1981) "evolutionary approach" to the iterated Prisoners' Dilemma game is not restricted by arbitrary limits placed upon the number of strategies available to the players. This approach, which considers all possible strategies, posits "the existence of a whole population of individuals employing a certain strategy, B, and a single mutant individual employing another strategy, A" (Axelrod, 1981: 310).

If the players in this game interact with each other one at a time, then it is possible that the expected payoff of an individual using strategy A is higher than the expected payoff of a member of the general population. In this case, strategy A is said to *invade* strategy B. But if the converse is true, and if no other strategy can invade B, B is said to be *collectively stable*.

Are there any conditions under which a cooperative strategy can invade a noncooperative strategy in an iterated Prisoners' Dilemma game? And are there any conditions under which a cooperative strategy is collectively stable in such a game?

To answer this question Axelrod, like Taylor, assumes a discount parameter, w—where $0 \le w \le 1$—that can be interpreted as before, or as an estimate that an individual player makes of the probability of encountering the same opponent in a future game. Thus, the smaller w is, the less important future payoffs become.

Interestingly, Axelrod proves that a tit-for-tat strategy that cooperates in the first game and then reciprocates the previous choice of the other player in each subsequent game—Taylor's (B) strategy—is a collectively stable strategy, provided that w is sufficiently large. Unfortunately, a strategy of selecting (D) on every play of the iterated Prisoners' Dilemma is *always* a collectively stable strategy, regardless of the value of w. This means that a population of unconditionally noncooperative players (called *meanies*) cannot be invaded by conditionally cooperative players arriving in the population one at a time.

To some extent, however, this dismal conclusion can be mitigated if newcomers arrive in clusters, rather than individually, and if the newcomers interact with each other more than they interact with members of the general population. As Axelrod shows, under these conditions a number of strategies *can* invade a world of meanies. Of those strategies that can invade a population of noncooperative players, *maximally discriminating strategies* require the smallest amount of interactions among members of the invading cluster.

A strategy is *maximally discriminating* if it will eventually cooperate even if the other has never cooperated yet, and once it cooperates it will never cooperate again with ALL D but will always cooperate with another player using the same strategy [Axelrod, 1981: 316].

Significantly, tit-for-tat is one such maximally discriminating strategy. From this and related results, Axelrod (1981: 317) concludes that

cooperation can emerge even in a world of unconditional defection. The development cannot take place if it is tried only by scattered individuals who have no chance to interact with each other. But cooperation can emerge from small clusters of discriminating individuals, as long as these individuals have even a small proportion of their interactions with each other. Moreover, if nice strategies (those which are never the first to defect) eventually come to be adopted by virtually everyone, then those individuals can afford to be generous in dealing with any others. The population of nice rules can also protect themselves against clusters of individuals using any other strategy just as well as they can protect themselves against single individuals. . . . So mutual cooperation can emerge in a world of egoists without central control, by starting with a cluster of individuals who rely on reciprocity.

This is a long way from the pessimistic conclusion reached at the beginning of this section, and confirms what was felt all along, namely that cooperation *is* rational in the indefinitely repeated Prisoners' Dilemma game. Nevertheless, because this result—and the result based on the notion of a nonmyopic equilibrium—depend upon a highly specific set of assumptions, it should sensitize us to the fact that cooperation is not automatic and may be difficult to achieve in the real world. Stated optimistically, these results suggest that mutual cooperation in a Prisoners' Dilemma situation is possible if players take a long-run view of things and consider the future consequences of their present actions. Unfortunately, in many situations, it seems that players take too seriously John Maynard Keynes's well-known dictum that in the long-run we will all be dead.

Concluding Comments

To some readers, the preceding discussion of nonzero-sum games may have been somewhat disappointing since no general solution concept, analogous to the Minimax Theorem for zero-sum games, was presented. As already indicated, the absence of such a solution concept for nonzero-sum games is due mainly to the fact that two or more nonequivalent or noninterchangeable equilibrium outcomes may exist, though it is also due to the possible nonexistence of a pure strategy equilibrium in these games.

The absence of a determinate solution for nonzero-sum games has some important implications for the suitability of game theory as a tool for social analysis. Since equilibrium outcomes represent stable points in the set of possible societal states, they can be expected to be selected by rational agents on a regular basis. Consequently, the identification of these regularly occurring outcomes in both the model world and the real world is a precondition to the discovery and specification of general laws of social behavior. Therefore, unless competing equilibria can be eliminated in situations wherein multiple equilibria are found, or unless specific equilibria can be discovered where none ostensibly exists, explanations and predictions derived from game-theoretic models will be weak and less than fully satisfying.

Some analysts have reacted to this prospect by abandoning altogether the notion of an equilibrium as a cornerstone of a theory of nonzero-sum games. The models they have developed, however, suffer from numerous difficulties.[25] And, as Luce and Raiffa (1957: 105) point out,

> even if it is possible to produce pathological examples which throw doubt upon the universality of a concept, this does not necessarily undermine its importance. It merely establishes that care must be exerted to check whether the concept is plausible in the specific cases to which it has been applied. Ideally, one should attempt to investigate the mathematical restrictions which should be placed on the domain of admissible games so that the concept is plausible. In the case of the equilibrium point concept for noncooperative games, we know that several major difficulties exist; nonetheless, it is an exceptionally important tool for the analysis of wide classes . . . of games.

In the spirit of Luce and Raiffa's comment, the more traditional response to the problems underlying the lack of a general solution concept for nonzero-sum games has been to attempt to generate a specific equilibrium or eliminate competing equilibria by either making stronger assumptions or incorporating additional environmental detail into more content-specific models that are, by necessity, absent in the more general formulations. The supposition beneath both of these research strategies is that the indeterminacy of some games may be eliminated by departing from the rarefied atmosphere of game-theoretic models devoid of real-world content. If this is so, then satisfying explanations and predictions are not precluded.

In this context it is worth noting that the discussion in the previous section of proposed solutions to the Prisoners' Dilemma can be thought of as an illustration of several ways that simple models can be modified or extended. Not only do these proposed solutions shed light on the conditions under which the tension between individuals and group rationality might be eliminated, but they also demonstrate several methods by which unadorned game-theoretic models might be altered to take into account the vagaries of specific environmental conditions.

One conclusion that might be drawn from all of this is that if the theory of games is to fully transcend its formal structure and evolve into a mature methodology for examining real-world interactions, the input of practicing social scientists, working in a wide variety of political, social, and economic contexts, is essential. Reinforcing this conclusion is the fact that indeterminacy is even more pervasive in n-person games, the subject of the next chapter.

4. N-PERSON GAMES

Introduction

The theoretical edifice of n-person games, where n $\geq$ 3, will be the final division of game theory examined in this essay. Games of this category are both quantitatively and qualitatively different from two-person games. As soon as a third player is added to a game, the possibility of a coalition between two of them arises. Thus it should not be surprising that the primary focus of n-person game theory has been on the dynamics of coalition formation and disintegration, and on the distribution of payoffs within coalitions. As will be seen, this justifiable concern with coalitions has resulted in an n-person theory that differs significantly, in both appearance and spirit, from the theory of two-person games.

A Three-Person Game:
The Geneva Conference of 1954

The simplest n-person games are, of course, three-person games. Although they may be simple, many scholars consider them the most important type of multiperson game. In addition to the fact that many significant political, economic, and social situations contain three players, there is also considerable opinion in the sociological literature that all larger groups can be reduced to triads (Caplow, 1968: 10). Thus it seems appropriate to begin this survey of n-person game theory with a real-life example of a three-person game. An examination of this game, called the Geneva Conference game of 1954, will also permit an illustration of some of the more obvious extensions of two-person game theory to the world of n-person games.

The Geneva Conference game, which marked the end of the Franco-Vietminh war, began to crystallize in late 1953. By the fall of that year, the Franco-Vietminh war was stalemated, and pressures began to mount on the French government to negotiate a settlement with the Vietminh. As the game progressed, the players began to cluster into three distinct coalitions: the Western Alliance, led and dominated by the United States, also included France and Great Britain; the Sino-Soviet bloc; and the single-member coalition, the Democratic Republic of Vietnam (the DRV or Vietminh).

When the Indochinese phase of the conference convened in May 1954, three alternatives faced the participants. The first was a stalemate that would result if the players resisted a settlement of any kind. If this occurred, the status quo would prevail and the war would continue.

(Both American and Vietminh officials believed that their side would eventually win this conflict.) A second possibility, proposed by the French, implied a partitioned Vietnam. The French wanted to limit the discussions at Geneva to military matters and delay negotiating a political settlement until after a cease-fire. The third alternative, proposed by the DRV, was to discuss military and political matters concurrently. All of the participants viewed this proposal as implying an immediate French withdrawal from Vietnam to be followed by a general election. As the U.S. Joint Chiefs of Staff concluded, this alternative "would be attended by almost certain loss of the Associated States to Communist control" (Pentagon Papers, 1971, 1:449).

In light of the preceding analysis, the following notation will be used to represent the set of alternatives $A = \{a_1, a_2, a_3\}$, where

a_1: the status quo, a continuation of the conflict;
a_2: a military solution probably resulting in a permanent partition of Vietnam; and
a_3: a military *and* political solution probably resulting in Ho Chi Minh's victory in a general election.

Given this set of alternatives, the preferences of each of the three coalitions at Geneva were as follows:

(1) the Western Alliance: (a_1, a_2, a_3);
(2) the Sino-Soviet bloc: (a_2, a_3, a_1);
(3) the Vietminh: (a_3, a_1, a_2).

Thus, in this representation, the Western Alliance (United States) most preferred a_1, next most preferred a_2, and least preferred a_3. The preference orders of the other two players are interpreted in the same way.[26]

At the Geneva Conference, the power relationships among the players dictated that decisions could be binding only by unanimous consent or by a coalition of two of the three players. Thus, the operating *decision rule* was this: If any two or more of the players agreed on one of the three alternatives, that alternative was the social choice. If there was no agreement and all three players disagreed, the status quo (a_1), would prevail.

The decision rule can be thought of as a function that assigns outcomes to an outcome matrix. To see this, assume for now that the Western Alliance always selects a strategy consistent with promoting the status quo (i.e., a_1). The possible outcomes of this game, given the

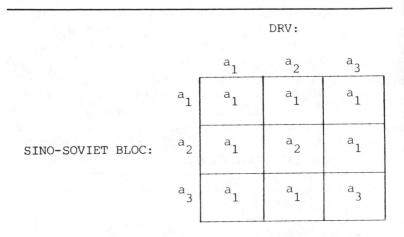

Figure 4.1 Outcome Matrix for the Geneva Conference Game of 1954, Given that the Western Alliance Selects Its Status Quo Strategy, a_1

choices of the other two players, are represented in the two-dimensional outcome matrix of Figure 4.1.

The first alternative, a_1, appears in seven of the nine cells of this matrix. In five of the seven cases, this alternative results from the selection of a strategy consistent with a_1 by two or more of the players. In the remaining two cases, at the intersection of the second column and the third row, and of the third column and the second row, a three-way split occurs. Since the decision rule stipulates that the status quo results when the players are unable to agree on a single outcome, a_1 is assigned to these two cells. Finally, the last two entries result when the Sino-Soviet bloc and the Vietminh agree on either a_2 or a_3.

If the assumption is dropped that the Western Alliance always selects a strategy consistent with a_1, the two-dimensional matrix of Figure 4.1 expands to the three-dimensional matrix represented in Figure 4.2. The only difference between these two figures is that the expanded matrix takes into account all three strategies of the Western Alliance. Hence, three planes instead of one are depicted in the expanded matrix.[27]

Outcomes are assigned to the expanded matrix in the same way they were assigned to the original matrix: by a function defined by the decision rule. For instance, if the Western Alliance selects a strategy consistent with a_2, and the Sino-Soviet bloc and the DRV select a strategy consistent with a_3, the outcome is a_3. Hence, in Figure 4.2, the outcome found at the intersection of the second plane, the third row, and the third column, indicated by an asterisk, is a_3.

What strategy should each player select to ensure the best possible outcome? The answer to this question depends upon the player's knowledge of the decision rule and of the preferences of the other players. If a player knows both the decision rule and the other players' preferences, he or she is said to possess *complete information*; otherwise, he or she possesses *incomplete information*.

If information is incomplete, a *sincere* strategy that is strictly consistent with a player's preferences is optimal, since a player without complete information would have no basis, other than preference order, on which to choose a strategy. For instance, a sincere strategy for the West would entail selecting a strategy associated with its most preferred alternative, a_1 (i.e., the first plane). Similarly, the sincere strategy for the Sino-Soviet bloc would be the choice associated with a_2 (the second row), and for the DRV a_3 (the third column).

The intersection of these three strategy choices (i.e., the first plane, the second row, and the third column) defines the sincere outcome. If all players select a sincere strategy, a three-way split occurs. Hence, the sincere outcome is a_1.

This particular sincere outcome, however, is not an equilibrium outcome. It is *vulnerable* to an insincere strategy by either the Sino-Soviet bloc or the DRV. For instance, if the Sino-Soviet bloc acted insincerely and selected a strategy consistent with its second best alternative, a_3, they would induce a_3, marked by a circle in Figure 4.2, rather than a_1. Since the Sino-Soviet bloc prefers a_3 to a_1, it would not be in its interest to use a sincere strategy in this game, given that the other players stick to their sincere strategy choices.

With incomplete information, however, the Sino-Soviet bloc would not be able to exploit the instability of the sincere outcome since it would have no basis to predict, and hence react to, the strategy choices of the other players. Given incomplete information, then, a sincere strategy remains a player's best.

What if information is complete? In this case, a *sophisticated* strategy is optimal for each player, provided that the other players are also sophisticated (Farquharson, 1969). A sophisticated strategy is arrived at by the successive elimination of dominated strategies by each player. If one strategy dominates all of a player's other strategies, it is said to be *straightforward*. A straightforward strategy is an unconditionally best strategy.

In the game outlined above, a_3 emerges as the sophisticated outcome, as is easily demonstrated. From Figure 4.2 it can be seen that both the Western Alliance and the DRV have straightforward strategies. For the West, the choice of its strategy "pursue a_1" (the first plane) is unconditionally best since it dominates both of its other two strategies. (To determine this, each outcome in the first plane, given a particular combination of strategy choices by the other two players, must be compared with each outcome in the second and third planes. For example, if the Sino-Soviet bloc pursues a_2 and the DRV pursues a_3, the outcome is a_1 if the West pursues a_1 and is a_2 if the West pursues a_2. Thus, in *this* instance, since the West prefers a_1 to a_2, its first strategy is better than its second. A similar analysis, comparing each of the remaining outcomes in the first and second planes would reveal that no matter what choices are made by the other players, the outcome resulting from the West's pursue a_1 strategy is either the same or better than the outcome resulting from its pursue a_2 strategy. This means that its first strategy dominates its second strategy.) Similarly, the DRV's choice of pursue a_3 is straightforward; it dominates both its first and second strategies.

By contrast, the Sino-Soviet bloc has no unconditionally best strategy. Its second strategy dominates it first but not its third. Therefore, the Sino-Soviet bloc's choice of a best strategy depends upon the other two players' choices.

If information is complete, each player will be able to determine which strategies of the other players are dominated. Since a dominated strategy is never better, and is sometimes worse, than a strategy that dominates it, it seems safe to assume that each player will limit its choices to the set of undominated strategies. Hence the dominated strategies of each player can be eliminated from further consideration.

With these strategies eliminated, Figure 4.2 reduces to Figure 4.3, where only the Sino-Soviet bloc has more than one strategy choice left. Since the Sino-Soviet bloc prefers the outcome associated with its third strategy, a_3, to the outcome associated with its second, a_1, its rational choice would be to pursue a_3 and thereby induce a_3 as the sophisticated outcome.[28]

The fact that a_3 is the sophisticated outcome is somewhat paradoxical. In the original outcome matrix, the Western Alliance can reach its first preference a_1 in almost twice as many ways as it can reach either of the other two alternatives. Ostensibly, while the West seems to be in the best tactical position, its worst outcome is adopted when all the players use sophisticated strategies.

Is there anything the Western Alliance could do to rectify this strategically unfavorable result? If the information is complete, the answer is "no." Sophisticated strategies are optimal given complete information; they cannot be improved upon if the other players are sophisticated. However, if the West could conceal its true preferences

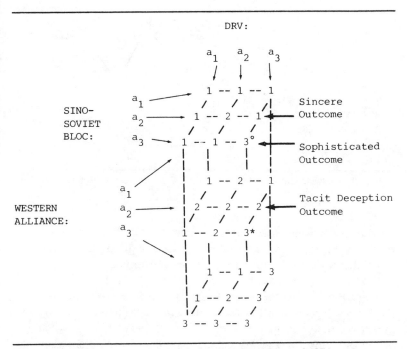

Figure 4.2 Outcome Matrix for the Geneva Conference Game of 1954

and somehow announce a false preference order which the other players believe, two additional strategies become available. First, after this announcement, the West could act as if this announcement were its true preference. This type of deceptive strategy is called *tacit deception* since other players cannot detect the deception unless they know the user's true preference order. The second option open to the West also entails making a false announcement but acting consistently with its true preferences. Since other players can easily detect an action that contradicts the deceiver's announced preference order, this strategy is called *revealed deception* (Brams and Zagare, 1977, 1981).

To illustrate how these deceptive strategies operate, assume the West announces its preference order to be (a_2, a_1, a_3) instead of (a_1, a_2, a_3). If the DRV and the Sino-Soviet bloc believe this (false) announcement, they perceive the West's second strategy (rather than its first) to be straightforward. Since their preferences remain constant, the un-dominated strategies of the DRV and the Sino-Soviet bloc remain as before.

After eliminating the West's (apparent) dominated strategies and the (actual) dominated strategies of the DRV and the Sino-Soviet bloc from

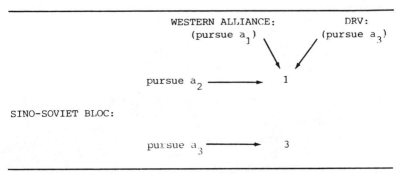

Figure 4.3 Reduced Outcome Matrix for the Geneva Conference Game, Given Complete Information

consideration, Figure 4.2 reduces to Figure 4.4. This figure is remarkably similar to Figure 4.3 except that now there is a different outcome (a_2) associated with the Sino-Soviet bloc's second strategy (pursue a_2).

Given the Sino-Soviet bloc's preference for a_2 over a_3, its rational strategy, if it believes the West's false announcement, is to pursue a_2. If the West acts consistently with its announcement and also chooses to pursue a_2, the (manipulated) sophisticated outcome is a_2, which is a better outcome for the West (and the Sino-Soviet bloc) than the (unmanipulated) sophisticated outcome a_3. Thus, the West has an incentive to deceive the other players tacitly.

There is some evidence that suggests that this is exactly what happened at Geneva (Zagare, 1979). By making a series of announcements indicating that it preferred a partitioned Vietnam (a_2) to continuing the conflict (a_1), the Western Alliance (the United States) tacitly deceived the Soviets, the Chinese, and the DRV and thereby induced a_2 as the (manipulated) sophisticated outcome. Its incentive to do so, therefore, explains "the obvious contrast between the public and private comments of the Eisenhower Administration officials and organs" that the authors of *The Pentagon Papers* (1971, 1: 177) discovered in reviewing the historical record of the Geneva Conference.

It is important to point out that the (manipulated) sophisticated outcome induced by the West's tacit deception is not stable with respect to its true preference order. By choosing its strategy pursue a_1, the West could have induced a_1 as the (manipulated) sophisticated outcome, which it preferred to the tacit-deception outcome. However, the West's choice of this strategy would have been inconsistent with its announced preference order. Since the other players would have easily observed this inconsistency, they would have detected the Western deception.

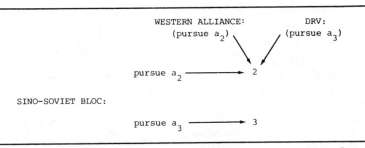

Figure 4.4   Reduced Outcome Matrix for the Geneva Conference Game, Given the
Western Alliance's False Announcement

The Characteristic Function Form of Representation

Sophisticated (and the related deception) strategies reviewed in the last section are motivated only by each player's awareness of the other player's preferences and the decision rule. Since they do not depend upon an ability of the players to negotiate binding agreements, they seem particularly relevant to situations in which there are obstacles (such as antitrust laws) that block explicit communication, or in which institutional mechanisms for enforcing contracts do not exist, as might be the case in the international system.

Games in which binding agreements are not possible are termed *noncooperative.* By contrast, *cooperative* games are those in which binding agreements are possible. For each of these categories of games, a separate and not totally unified theory has evolved. Up to this point, however, the analysis in this book has been entirely from the vantage point of the noncooperative theory, since most of the interesting interactive problems and applications are highlighted by this perspective. Moreover, for two-person games, at least, the noncooperative theory is more fully developed than the corresponding cooperative theory.[29]

This, however, ceases to be true in the analysis of n-person games. The noncooperative approach of the last section is atypical of n-person game theory. Most theoretical and empirical studies of the n-person problem have been approached from a cooperative perspective. More specifically, n-person game theory generally begins with the assumption that there are no rules that prohibit players from negotiating binding agreements.

Associated with this assumption are two related assumptions. First, it is generally assumed that "side-payments" are permitted. This simply means that members of a winning coalition are able to distribute the payoffs that accrue to the coalition. Second, utility is usually assumed to be "unrestrictedly transferable." As Luce and Raiffa (1957: 168) put it, this assumption supposes

> that there exists an infinitely divisible, real, and desirable commodity (which for all the world behaves like money) such that any reapportionment of it among the players results in increments and decrements of individual utilities which sum to zero according to some specific set of utility scales for the players.

Neither of these assumptions, of course, is necessary. They are simplifying assumptions that have provided useful starting points for the development of n-person game theory. Like so many other assumptions used by game theorists, they can be relaxed as demanded by the situation being modeled.

In addition to the noncooperative perspective, there is a second way that the discussion of sophisticated strategies in the previous section is atypical of n-person game theory, namely, the use of the normal form to represent the strategic structure of the game. The normal form is generally eschewed in the analysis of n-person games because it becomes almost impossible to conceptualize, or depict, for games among four or more players. Moreover, the complexities increase exponentially as n increases.

To simplify the representation of n-person games, von Neumann and Morgenstern developed the notion of a *characteristic function*. The characteristic function abstracts the essential features of these games (i.e., those most germane to the process of coalition formation) by assigning a value to every possible coalition. The assignment of a value, or payoff, to a coalition is based upon the assumption that each coalition is faced with the worst possible strategic situation. For instance, suppose that in an n-person zero-sum game a coalition, say S, forms. In this case, the members of S could coordinate their individual strategies in order to maximize their joint payoffs. The payoffs to this coalition, however, will be kept to a minimum if the countercoalition of all the remaining players, -S (in set-theoretic terminology, the complement of S) forms and the members of -S coordinate their individual strategies. The formation of -S, therefore, is the worst strategic situation for S, and the original game is, in effect, reduced to a two-person zero-sum game between S and -S.

As was seen in Chapter 2, each player in a two-person zero-sum game maximizes its security level and assures itself the value, v, of a game by selecting a maximin or a minimax strategy. Since S can do no worse than v, (though it may in fact do better if -S does not form), it is this payoff that is assigned to S by the characteristic function. Put in a slightly different way, the characteristic function assigns to each coalition the payoff associated with the (joint) strategy that maximizes its security level.

To be sure, the characteristic function rests upon a conservative, and descriptively dubious, assumption. In many games, especially of the nonzero-sum variety, the worst case scenario is not likely to be realized. For instance, as Olson (1965) has shown, (counter)coalitions can be expected to form only under extremely limited conditions. (Witness the absence of an effective counter-coalition to OPEC in the early 1970s.) These conditions are less likely to be satisfied, all things being equal, as the number of players in a game increases.

Still, this assumption can be defended on pragmatic grounds. It provides a useful starting point for the analysis of n-person games, and it permits a parsimonious representation of the strategic structure of these games. Without this, or an analogous, simplifying assumption, the analysis of n-person games would probably be well-nigh impossible.

Formally, the characteristic function, v, is defined to be a real-valued function that satisfies the following conditions:

$$v(\phi) = 0, \text{ where } \phi \text{ is the empty set (coalition), and} \qquad [4.1]$$

$$v(S \cup T) \geq v(S) + v(T), \text{ where S and T are any two} \qquad [4.2]$$
nonoverlapping (disjoint) players or coalitions.

The first condition, a technical restriction, merely states that a coalition with no members has no value. The second condition, known as *superadditivity*, requires that the payoff to a coalition between two players (or coalitions), S and T, be at least as good, and perhaps better, than the payoff S and T receive as separate coalitions or individuals.

Of course, superadditivity does not hold for all n-persons games. Such games are termed *inessential* and are of little intrinsic interest since "there is no occasion for any strategy of coalitions, no element of struggle or competition" (von Neumann and Morgenstern: 1953, 249). Conversely, games for which the inequality condition of statement 4.2 is satisfied for some coalitions are called *essential*. In this chapter, only essential games will be considered.

In addition to 4.1 and 4.2, the characteristic function of zero-sum games satisifies two additional conditions:

$$v(S) = -v(-S), \text{and} \qquad [4.3]$$
$$v(I_n) = 0 \text{ where } I_n \text{ is the grand coalition of all the players.} \qquad [4.4]$$

Condition 4.3 is satisfied because the security level of each player or coalition in a zero-sum game is exactly the opposite of the security level of the other remaining player or coalition. And 4.4 reflects the fact that in a zero-sum game, each player extracts its payoff from the other player(s). If the grand coalition forms, and the countercoalition is empty, there is no wealth for the grand coalition to expropriate.

The Core

Though the characteristic function is based upon a somewhat conservative assumption, a player contemplating joining one of several coalitions might find the information contained therein useful. The characteristic function tells such a player what could happen in the worst possible contingency should it join a particular coalition. In this way, it reflects the underlying strategic structure of a game.

Given this structure, it is natural to ask how the players will divide the value of a game and whether the information contained in the characteristic function has any particular implications for which coalition will actually form. In the context of n-person (cooperative) game theory, the answer to one or both of these questions consitutes a solution. (Notice that this notion of a solution differs from that associated with noncooperative game theory, where the emphasis is on identifying optimal strategies and stable outcomes.) A number of solution concepts for n-person, cooperative, games exist in the literature.[30] In the next two sections, two of the most prominent solution concepts— the core and the V-solution—will be examined.

Both the core and the V-solution, as well as many other solution concepts, rest upon the idea of an *imputation*. An imputation is a member of that subset of logically possible payoff configurations that satisfy both the condition of individual and of group rationality (to be defined presently).

More formally, let x_i represent the payoff to player i, and let the vector (or n-tuple of real numbers) $X = (x_1, x_2, \ldots, x_n)$ represent a particular disbursement of the value of a game to each of the n players in it. There are, of course, an infinitely large number of X's (i.e., payoff configurations) in some games. Not all of these X's, however, are equally defensible. Some of these potential societal states may be eliminated, a priori, by rational players. For instance, it is hard to imagine that any player would accept a payoff that is less than its security level, or what can be guaranteed as given by the characteristic function, that is, $v(\{i\})$. Hence, one would expect that any distribution of the value of the game would satisfy the condition of *individual rationality*:

$$x_i \geq v(\{i\}) \qquad [4.5]$$

Similarly, one would not expect the group of n players to accept less than what it could guarantee itself. This is the condition of *group rationality* or Pareto-optimality:

$$\sum_{i \text{ in } I_n} x_i = v(I_n) \qquad [4.6]$$

Briefly, the justification for 4.6 is this: Suppose that after dividing up the value of a game, there is some amount, say w, left over. This means that

$$\sum_{i \text{ in } n} x_i \leq v(I_n)$$

One, or some, or all of the players would be better off, and no one worse off, if w were distributed. Consequently, one would expect the group, or some part of it, to consume w.

As already indicated, any payoff vector satisfying 4.5 and 4.6 is termed an imputation. An imputation can be thought of as a possible social arrangement that satisfies minimal conditions of rationality. Presumably, any ultimate arrangement will be drawn from the set of imputations. This is why Shubik (1982: 141) has argued that the set of imputations is "the territory over which the coalitions do battle." Which imputation is finally selected depends upon which winning coalition forms.

But the set of imputations may itself be quite large. Are there any conditions, in addition to individual and group rationality, that might reasonably be imposed on the set of payoff configurations? Some theorists have argued that the condition of *coalition rationality* is a natural extension of the conditions of individual and group rationality. Coalition rationality requires that the security level of every coalition be satisfied, or that

$$\sum_{i \text{ in } S} x_i \geq v(S), \text{ for all } S \text{ in } I_n \qquad [4.7]$$

In words, 4.7 stipulates that the sum of the payoffs to each of the players in *any* coalition S in a game be at least as good as the payoff guaranteed that coalition by the characteristic function.

The rationale behind 4.7 is this. Suppose that some coalition, say T, forms and attempts to divide the value assigned T by the characteristic function. Further suppose that a subgroup of T, say S, is offered a payoff less than what S is worth according to the characteristic function. In this case, S would not (rationally) accept the offer since it can do better without the remaining members of T. Thus, for S to remain in any coalition, it would have to receive at least as much as v(S). If this argument is extended to all possible conditions, then the condition of coalition rationality is required.

The set of imputations satisfying the condition of coalition rationality constitutes the *core*. Alternatively, the core may be defined as the set of *undominated imputations*. Technically, one imputation, X, *dominates* another imputation, Y, with respect to some nonempty coalition, S—called the *effective set*—if the following two conditions are met:

$$(1) \quad \sum_{i \text{ in } S} x_i \leq v(S), \text{ and}$$

$$(2) \quad x_i > y_i \text{ for all i in S}$$

The first condition requires that X be feasible in the sense that the members of S can obtain the amount implied by X to distribute among themselves; and the second condition requires that *every* member of S receive a better payoff if the distribution implied by X is made than they would receive if the distribution implied by Y is made.

Because it contains only undominated imputations, the core is an extremely attractive solution concept,[31] for no individual or group has both the opportunity and the incentive to overturn a societal arrangement if the imputation arrived at is in the core. In other words, given the strategic structure of a game, as defined by the characteristic function, the demands of every player and of every coalition can be satisfied. Imputations in the core, then, are particularly stable.

Unfortunately, for the purpose of specifying a general solution for n-person games, the core has one major deficiency: In many games it does not exist. It is easy to show that all essential constant-sum games have an empty core. Many nonconstant-sum games also lack a core. For example, Rubinstein (1979) has proved that if only continuous preferences are assumed, majority voting games will not have a core. The Geneva Conference game of 1954 is a specific example of a game without a core.

To see this, recall that three players and their preferences over the set of alternatives were as follows:

(1)   Western Alliance: (a_1, a_2, a_3);

(2)   Sino-Soviet bloc: (a_2, a_3, a_1);

(3)   DRV: (a_3, a_1, a_2).

If only ordinal and, hence, nontransferable utilities are assumed, and if a value of 3 is assigned to each player's best alternative, 2 to each player's next-best alternative, and 1 to each player's worst alternative, then, if a_1 is the outcome, the imputation $X = (3, 1, 2)$ results, where the first entry represents the payoff to the West, the second the payoff to the Sino-Soviet bloc, and the last entry the payoff to the DRV. Thus, if a_1 is selected, the West realizes its best, the Sino-Soviet bloc its worst, and the DRV its next-best outcome. Similarly, if a_2 is selected, the imputation $Y = (2, 3, 1)$ results; and if a_3 is selected, the imputation $Z = (1, 2, 3)$ results. X, Y, and Z exhaust the set of imputations.

It is easy to see that each of these imputations is dominated by another:

(a) $X = (3, 1, 2)$ is dominated by $Z = (1, 2, 3)$ with respect to a coalition between the Sino-Soviet bloc and the DRV;

(b) $Y = (2, 3, 1)$ is dominated by $X = (3, 1, 2)$ with respect to a coalition between the Western Alliance and the DRV; and

(c) $Z = (1, 2, 3)$ is dominated by $Y = (2, 3, 1)$ with respect to a coalition between the Western Alliance and the DRV.

Thus, the Geneva Conference game lacked a core.

This example also shows that the dominance relationship is not, in general, transitive. It is possible for one imputation, X, to dominate another, Y, with respect to one coalition; for Y to dominate Z with respect to another; and for Z to dominate X with respect to still another coalition.

The fact that the Geneva Conference game lacked a core can be thought of as an alternate explanation for the motivation of the Western Alliance to tacitly deceive the other players at the conference. Given a false announcement of its preferences by the Western Alliance, the game played at Geneva appeared to be defined by the following preference orders:

Western Alliance: (a_2, a_1, a_3);
Sino-Soviet bloc: (a_2, a_3, a_1);
DRV: (a_3, a_1, a_2).

These preferences give rise to the following set of imputations:

$a_1 \rightarrow X = (2, 1, 2)$;

$a_2 \rightarrow Y = (3, 3, 1);$

$a_3 \rightarrow Z = (1, 2, 3).$

It is easy to see that Y dominates both X and Z with respect to an alliance between the West and the Sino-Soviet bloc, and that Y is undominated by any other imputation. Y, therefore, defines the core. (Although the DRV prefers both X and Z to Y, the payoffs to the DRV in both of these coalitions are not feasible, that is, given the decision rule, the DRV cannot achieve either of these payoffs as a single-member coalition.) Thus, given the Western deception, the coalition between the Western Alliance and the Sino-Soviet bloc (i.e., Y) could no longer be upset by the DRV. The actual outcome of the Geneva Conference game can therefore be supported by either the noncooperative or the cooperative variant of n-person game theory.

The existence or nonexistence of a core is arguably the most important characteristic of an n-person game. Games that have a core or, like the Geneva Conference game, appear to have a core, are likely to evolve in a predictable and determinate way once (and if) an imputation in the core is reached. On the other hand, games without a core are more problematic; and since they are more fluid, are perhaps more interesting. Games without a core are likely to be characterized by perpetual flux, as unsatisfied coalition after unsatisfied coalition attempts to overturn the existing order.[32] Understanding this process is a question of immense importance to social science. To get a better handle on it, we will wade a little further into the theory of n-person games.

The von Neumann-Morgenstern V-Solution

Von Neumann and Morgenstern were fully cognizant of the possibility that some games might have an empty core. Hence, in their initial attempt to define a solution for n-person cooperative games, they did not impose the requirement—defining the core—that an imputation in a solution satisfy the condition of coalition rationality (4.7). Instead, they focused on identifying *sets, S,* of imputations such that

no imputation X in *S* is dominated by any other
imputation Y in *S*, and   [4.8]

any imputation Z not in *S* is dominated by at least
one imputation X in *S*.   [4.9]

Von Neumann and Morgenstern termed any set of imputations satisfying 4.8 and 4.9 a solution—hereafter, a V-solution—and thought of each V-solution as a "standard of behavior" that operated on a segment of society. The first restriction ensured that each standard was "free from inner contradictions"; and the second restriction guaranteed that each standard could "be used to discredit any non-conforming procedure," that is, any imputation or distribution of the value of the game not implied by S. Thus, sets of imputations that meet the requirements of a V-solution

> have an inner stability: once they are generally accepted they overrule everything else and no part of them can be overruled within the limits of the accepted standards [von Neumann and Morgenstern, 1953: 41-42].

To illustrate the V-solution with an example, consider a three-person game with the following characteristic function:

$$v(1) = v(2) = v(3) = -1$$
$$v(1,2) = v(1,3) = v(2,3) = 1$$
$$v(1,2,3) = 0$$

Von Neumann and Morgenstern (1953: 222-223) refer to this game as "Couples." Couples is a three-person, zero-sum game in which any two player coalition can extract one unit of utility from the excluded player.

Like Prisoner's Dilemma and Chicken, Couples is a generic game common to interactions at all levels of social, political, and economic life. Nevertheless, its constant-sum characteristics render this game particularly germane to the political world. As Riker and Ordeshook (1973: 124) have put it, Couples is

> the quintessence of politics. . . . The heart of politics is people choosing each other either implicitly or explicitly—that is, forming groups, parties, factions, coalitions, alliances, ententes, and so on, every one of which involves choosing up sides. All the bargaining, negotiating, maneuvering, wheeling and dealing, ideologizing, philosophizing, persuading, rhetoricizing, and the like that characterize politics—all this is the preface to choosing, the artistic elaboration on the fundamental political action. Couples, as the abstract form of choosing up sides, is therefore the most elementary model of politics.

It is easy to show that the following set of imputations, A, is one V-solution of Couples:

$$\{X = (\tfrac{1}{2}, \tfrac{1}{2}, -1); \ Y = (\tfrac{1}{2}, -1, \tfrac{1}{2}); \ Z = (-1, \tfrac{1}{2}, \tfrac{1}{2})\}$$

First, notice that no imputation in A is dominated by any other imputation in A. To see this, compare, for instance, X with Y. Player 1 is indifferent between X and Y. Player 2 prefers X to Y but player 3 prefers Y to X. With respect to any two-player coalition—i.e., (1,2), (1,3), or (2,3)—at most, only one player will prefer X to Y or Y to X.[33] Hence, neither X nor Y dominates the other. A similar argument applies to the relationship between X and Z and between Y and Z. Since this exhausts the possibilities, 4.8 is satisfied. Second, A also satisfies 4.9. Any imputation not in A is dominated by *some* imputation in A.[34]

This solution has a certain intuitive appeal. The set A is internally stable. If an imputation in A is reached, there is no incentive to move to another imputation in A, since the elements of A do not dominate each other. A is also externally stable. Since every imputation not in A is dominated by some imputation in A, outside imputations, while possibly attractive initially, are not stable.

Unfortunately, despite its appealing features, the V-solution, like the core, suffers from some disabling pathologies. First of all, V-solutions are not necessarily unique. Indeed, most games have many V-solutions, and for some games an infinity of V-solutions exists. Worse still, it is even possible—for instance, in three-person zero-sum games like Couples—for *every* imputation to be in some V-solution. In such games, therefore, the V-solution is tautologically true. And, as Lucas (1968, 1969) has shown, not all games have V-solutions.

Von Neumann and Morgenstern, aware of all these difficulties except the last, were not chagrined. They argued that each of the possibly infinite number of V-solutions represented different "standards of behavior." The particular standard operative in a game milieu would determine which set of imputations would emerge and be selected by the players. For example, in Couples, if a norm existed that required that winners and losers be treated equally, and that their payoffs depend only upon whether they won or lost and not on their position in society, then one of the imputations in A, an example of a *nondiscriminatory solution*, would be selected.

On the other hand, if a norm existed that fixed the payoff of one or some of the players at either a positive or negative level then a *discriminatory* solution of the form

$$\{(x_1, x_2, c); \ (x_1, c, x_3); \ (c, x_2, x_3)\}$$

where c is some constant, would be selected. Societal norms, taboos, and customs would determine both the value of c and the player singled out for discriminatory treatment.

One is left with an empty feeling. As Shubik (1982: 162) has pointed out, the V-solution

> does not predict a standard of behavior. Nor does it predict an outcome when the standard of behavior is known. Rather, it tells us whether a given set of social or economic procedures is stable, by investigating the domination properties of the set of imputations they give rise to. We can only get something approaching a prediction from this branch of game theory when we are able to discern some general properties enjoyed by all stable sets of the game.

Two responses to the indeterminacy of the V-solution (and the core) can be made. First, different or more restrictive logical conditions could be imposed on the set of payoff configurations or imputations in order to generate an ideally unique equilibrium for all n-person games. As indicated, a number of other solution concepts, which in essence do just this, exist. For the most part, though, they suffer from defects similar to those exhibited by the V-solution and the core. Consequently, while the logical properties of these solutions are of interest to mathematicians, they have very little to offer working social scientists.

It is perhaps not surprising that very abstract game-theoretic models have been of limited use for theorizing about social interaction. Devoid of psychological, sociological, or structural information, these models ignore precisely those features of the real world—e.g., socialization patterns, socioeconomic hierarchies, societal norms, power distributions, economic or political arrangements, and so on—that social scientists argue are the most important determinants of human behavior. Thus it should also not be surprising that a second response to the indeterminacy of more general game-theoretic formulations has been to develop models that, by way of assumption, take into account the most salient characteristics of the milieu in which real-world players make decisions. Such models—e.g., of electoral competition, group behavior, market performance, and interstate conflict—abound in the social sciences today.[35] In general, these applications and extensions of n-person game theory have provided important insights into various aspects of social behavior. Two examples will be given next.

The Theory of Minimal Winning Coalitions

The focus of William Riker's (1962b) "solution" to n-person games is different from that of more conventional solution concepts. Whereas the core, the V-solution, and related notions seek to identify stable payoff configurations, Riker's solution consists of an answer to the question, "What size will winning coalitions be?"

Riker's answer begins with four standard assumptions of n-person cooperative game theory: that players are rational, that they have both perfect and complete information, that side-payments are permitted, and that the game is zero-sum. Riker also makes several "sociological" assumptions:

(1) Winning coalitions have positive value; losing or blocking coalitions have negative or zero-value.

(2) The primary goal of the players is to form winning coalitions.

(3) Winning coalitions are associated with imputations in which all members receive positive payoffs.

(4) Members of a winning coalition have control over its membership so that they can increase the size at will (Riker and Ordeshook, 1973: 179-180).

Given these assumptions, Riker attempts to deduce the optimal size of a coalition by examining the characteristic function at the point at which it is of minimal winning size, that is, just large enough to win. At this point the characteristic function may be decreasing, constant, or increasing.

In the case of a decreasing characteristic function, a minimal winning coalition clearly has no incentive to add additional members. If, under these circumstances, a coalition increased its size past the point at which it was minimally winning, not only would the value of the game divided up by the coalition be smaller, but this smaller value would have to be shared by more players. Similarly, should a coalition larger than minimal winning size form under these conditions, it will always be to the advantage of some members of the coalition to expel superfluous members so that fewer players can divide up a larger payoff.

If the value of the characteristic function remains constant past the minimal winning point, the inclusion of unnecessary members means that the winnings must be divided up among more players if the unnecessary players are not ejected. Hence, as in the previous case, a minimal winning coalition has no incentive to expand in size, and an incentive exists for oversized coalitions to eliminate players until the coalition is minimally winning.

What if the value of the characteristic function is increasing past the minimal winning point? Clearly, in this case a coalition will expand in order to expropriate the additional value. Nevertheless, as Riker and Ordeshook (1973: 184) point out,

> it is doubtful if this case ever exists in the real world, at least in zero-sum situations.... For instances of this case to occur, it must happen that players, *who know for sure that they have won,* nevertheless keep on acquiring additional adherents.

Note that because Riker does not believe in the existence of this case, he defines it out of existence. By assumption, since the primary goal of the players is to form a winning coalition, *all* value accrues to a coalition once it wins. This means that no value can be added to a coalition once the minimal winning point is reached.

Because each winning coalition is assigned a positive value (assumption 1), such coalitions have an incentive to form. But, as just illustrated, given the other assumptions of the model, there are no circumstances wherein an incentive exists for a coalition to grow beyond minimal winning size. These considerations give rise to a "sociological law" that Riker (1962b: 32) calls the *size principle*:

> *In n-person, zero-sum games, where side-payments are permitted, where the players are rational, and where they have perfect information, only minimal winning coalitions occur.*

It is important to point out that the set of assumptions provide limiting conditions for the operation of the size principle. When these conditions are not met, either the size principle does not apply, or its conclusions must be modified to take into account the changed circumstances. For example, one would not expect minimal winning coalitions necessarily to occur in nonzero-sum games since it may be the case in these games that the value of the characteristic function increases past the minimal winning point.

Of all the assumptions associated with the size principle, the assumption of complete and perfect information is perhaps the one least likely to be satisfied. Acknowledging this, Riker argues that players— uncertain about either the point at which a coalition is minimally winning, or whether or not a particular coalition is winning—will expand their coalitions past minimal winning size in order to increase the probability that they win. This propensity he calls the *information effect*. Thus Riker concludes that coalitions in the real world *tend* toward minimal winning size but do not actually attain it. It is this tendency statement, rather than the formal statement of the size principle, that Riker and others have attempted to verify.

Since the publication of *The Theory of Political Coalitions,* Riker's model has undergone extensive theoretical elaboration and been subjected to numerous—mostly supporting—empirical tests. Rather than review this large literature,[36] it would perhaps be more instructive to demonstrate the explanatory power of Riker's model by examining the aftermath of the election of 1824, a case that Riker offers as corroborating evidence for its validity.

In that election, since none of the four candidates for president received a majority of electoral votes, the election was thrown into the House of Representatives where each of the 24 states then in the Union had one vote. After some initial maneuvering, support for each candidate was as follows:

> John Quincy Adams: 10 votes;
>
> Andrew Jackson: 7 votes;
>
> William Crawford: 4 votes;
>
> Henry Clay: 3 votes.

The Twelfth Amendment limits the number of candidates in the House to the three with the highest number of electoral votes. Clay was eliminated on this count. But to whom should he throw his support? If he supported Jackson, Clay would create a deadlock between Adams and Jackson and, in effect, make Crawford kingmaker. On the other hand, if he instructed his supporters to back Adams, Adams would have exactly the majority needed to win. (Note that this is the coalition predicted by Riker's model.) For this, Clay had a price that Adams was apparently willing to pay. In return for his vote, Clay was designated Secretary of State in the so-called corrupt bargain of 1825. Riker and Ordeshook (1973: 200-201) made the following interpretation of the agreement reached by Adams and Clay:

> Many institutional forces, personal idiosyncrasies, and so on were doubtless involved in bringing about this outcome. It is interesting,

however, that it is exactly the outcome that is the rational best advantage for Adams and Clay. The bargain of 1825 may have seemed corrupt (especially to Jackson men), and Randolph of Roanoke called it an alliance between "puritan and blackleg" between "Blifil and Black George." Nevertheless it also appears rationally best to those who have the power to bring it about, and from this perspective of history, therefore, it appears natural.

The Shapley Value and the Power Index

Another solution that has received considerable attention from social scientists is the value solution proposed by L. S. Shapley (1953). Shapley's solution should be thought of as a measure of what a player can expect to get from a game. In this respect it resembles the value of a two-person zero-sum game (see Chapter 2).

There are times when a player might find information of this sort useful. For instance, such information might be helpful to a player who has an option whether or not to play a game, as when new constitutions or institutional arrangements are proposed. Under these circumstances a disadvantaged player might opt not to participate. Similarly, a player in an ongoing game might well wish to determine the biases of that game. When at an advantage, he or she might decide to resist attempts to overturn the existing order; and when in an inferior position, he or she might wish to change the rules of the game. In either case, however, a mechanism for evaluating a player's expected payoff is required. The *Shapley value* is one such measure.

Shapley's measure of value assumes that a player's expected payoff is a function of the incremental or marginal contribution he or she makes to every possible coalition in a game, weighted by the probability that each coalition will occur. In the absence of reasonable criteria by which to estimate this probability, Shapley assumes that the formation of every coalition is equiprobable.

To illustrate the calculation of the Shapley value, consider the following *weighted majority game* defined by a simple majority (i.e., 50 percent plus 1) decision rule and also by three players, 1, 2, and 3 with the following weights:

$$w_1 = 1, w_2 = 49, \text{ and } w_3 = 50,$$

where the weights represent the number of votes each player has in a voting game. To simplify the subsequent calculation, assume that the characteristic function assigns a value of 1 to a winning coalition and a value of 0 to a losing coalition. (Such games are called *simple games.*)

Given this assumption, the characteristic function of the weighted majority game is:

$$v(\phi) = 0$$

$$v(1) = v(2) = v(3) = 0$$

$$v(1,2) = 0; \ v(1,3) = v(2,3) = 1$$

$$v(1,2,3) = 1$$

In determining a value for each player, Shapley assumes that the grand coalition will form. In an n-person game, there are n! (read n factorial) different sequences in which this is possible. Hence, in the three-person weighted game, the grand coalition could form in 3! = 6 different ways:[37]

a. (1,2,3*)   b. (1,3*,2)   c. (2,1,3*)
d. (2,3*,1)   e. (3,1*,2)   f. (3,2*,1)

(Ignore for now the asterisks.) Hence the probability that any one of the six coalitions will actually form is $\frac{1}{6}$.

Consider now the marginal contribution made by Player 1, the player with 1 vote, if the first sequence (a) should occur. The marginal contribution of player 1 is measured by the value each coalition, S, has after 1 joins, less the value of S before 1 joins, or by

$$[v(S) - v(S - 1)]$$

In the first sequence, player 1 in effect joins a coalition that consists only of that player. Such a coalition, from the characteristic function, has a value of 0. Before 1 joined, the empty coalition, ϕ, which also has a value of 0, can be said to have existed. Hence, in this case the marginal contribution of the one-vote player:

$$[v(1) - v(\phi)] = (0 - 0) = 0$$

Applying this same logic to each of the six possible orderings gives rise to the Shapley value for player 1:

$$V_i = \frac{1}{6}[v(1) - v(\phi)] + \frac{1}{6}[v(1) - v(\phi)] + \frac{1}{6}[v(49,1) - v(49)]$$
$$+ \frac{1}{6}[v(49,50,1) - v(49,50)] + \frac{1}{6}[v(50,1) - v(50)]$$
$$+ \frac{1}{6}[v(50,49,1) - v(50,49)]$$

Factoring out the 1/6 term, i.e., the probability that each coalition will form, and substituting the value of each coalition gives

$$V_1 = \frac{1}{6}[(0-0) + (0-0) + (0-0) + (1-1) + (1-0) + (1-1)] = \frac{1}{6}$$

Similar calculations reveal that $V_2 = \frac{1}{6}$ and $V_3 = \frac{2}{3}$, which gives rise to the *value vector* $(\frac{1}{6}, \frac{1}{6}, \frac{2}{3})$.

Interestingly, the Shapley value for the player with 49 votes is exactly the same as that of the player with 1 vote, while the 50-vote player is assigned four times the value of either of the other two players. (A justification for the nonlinear relationship between a player's proportion of votes and that player's Shapley value will be given shortly.)

Shapley's value measure for n-person games possesses a number of attractive characteristics. First, notice that the sum of the values assigned to each player equals the value of the grand coalition, which in simple games is 1. This can be shown to be true in general. Second, the Shapley value is "symmetric" and hence does not depend upon the way the players are labeled. This means that the Shapley value is the same for players who are in identical strategic positions, and is different for players who are not. (One could hardly expect a satisfactory measure of value to be otherwise.) Finally, the Shapley value for a composite game, comprised of two separate games, is equal to the value of the two separate games.

Not only does the Shapley value satisfy these three conditions, but it is also the *only* measure of value that does. As Brams (1975: 162) has pointed out, "in the social sciences it is both rare and gratifying that an index, applicable to real-life situations . . . can be uniquely defined by an apparently reasonable set of conditions that it satisfies."

A special case of the Shapley value is the Shapley-Shubik (1954) index of voting power, also called the "power index." Intended as an a priori measure of voting power, the power index of player i, ϕ_i, is defined to be the number of times player i *pivots* (p_i) divided by the total number of pivots (n!) in a game, or

$$\phi_i = p_i / n!$$

A pivot is defined to be the player who turns a nonwinning coalition into a winning coalition. The position occupied by the pivot is called the *pivotal position.*

To illustrate these concepts, consider again the six possible sequences in which the grand coalition could form in the weighted majority game. In each of these orderings, the pivotal position is indicated by an asterisk. For example, in sequence a—in which the 1-vote player starts, followed by the 49-vote player, and finally by the 50-vote player—the 50-vote player is the pivot since the coalition between the 1- and 49-vote players is nonwinning while the grand coalition is a winning coalition. (Recall that a simple majority decision rule was assumed.) Since there are n! = 6 different ways in which the grand coalition could form, there are 6 pivots in this game. Of these 6 pivots, w_1 with 1 vote and w_2 with 49 votes are each in the pivotal position one time, while w_3 (the 50-vote player) is the pivot in four sequences. Hence,

$$\phi_1 = 1/6 \qquad\qquad \phi_{49} = 1/6 \qquad\qquad \phi_{50} = 2/3$$

which is the same as the Shapley value for this game.

This means that the Shapley value can also be interpreted as a measure of each player's "pivotalness," that is, the proportion of times a player's vote will be decisive. The higher this proportion, the higher will be the player's expected payoff or voting power. This measure of pivotalness (or decisiveness) corresponds to a common-sense appreciation of the notion of "power," at least in voting bodies.[38]

Though both the Shapley value and the power index may appear common-sensical, several nonobvious conclusions about voting power are revealed by the properties associated with it. For instance, in their original exposition of the power index, Shapley and Shubik (1954: 790) showed that

1. In pure *bi*cameral systems using simple majority votes, each chamber gets 50% of the power . . . regardless of the relative sizes. With more than two chambers, power varies inversely with size.
2. The power division in a multicameral system also depends on the type of majority required to pass a bill. Raising the majority in *one* chamber . . . increases the relative power of that chamber. Raising the required majority in all chambers simultaneously weakens the smaller house or houses at the expense of the larger.

A number of "paradoxes" of power have also been discovered in applications of the power index:[39]

The Paradox of New Members. Under certain conditions, when a new member is added to a weighted voting body, the power of one or more of the original members may actually *increase* (Brams and Affuso, 1976).

The Paradox of Quarreling Members. Under certain conditions, a quarrel between two members of a weighted voting body may increase the power of the quarreling members (Kilgour, 1974).

The Paradox of Large Size. Under certain conditions, a coalition between two or more members of a weighted voting body may actually decrease the share of voting power that members of the coalition have (Brams, 1975: 176-178).

The power index has been used to study the power distributions of a large number of real-world voting bodies.[40] Perhaps the most interesting empirical study concerns the apportionment of power in the legislature of Nassau County, New York, which has had a weighted voting system since 1957. In 1964 the weights of the six towns represented in the legislature were as follows: Hempstead (No. 1) and Hempstead (No. 2), 31 votes each; Oyster Bay, 28 votes, North Hempstead, 21 votes; and Glen Cove and Long Beach, 2 votes each. These weights give rise to the power vector (1/3, 1/3, 1/3, 0, 0, 0).

It is quite remarkable that all the power in this game resides with the three largest towns, and that the three towns with the smallest weights are afforded no power (technically, they are called *dummies*) by the power index. Since the representatives of each of the three smallest towns could never pivot, the voters in these towns were in effect disenfranchised by the system. As Banzhaf (1965: 339) argued,

> This analysis presents a very striking illustration of the dangers of assuming that an allocation of votes among representatives in proportion to population will automatically produce substantially equal representation for all citizens. It is hard to conceive of any theory of representative government which could justify a system under which the representatives of three of the six municipalities "represented" are allowed to attend meetings and cast votes, but are unable to have any effect on legislative decisions. Yet this is exactly what occurs now in Nassau County.

Fortunately, because Banzhaf discovered this anomaly, a new voting system was introduced in Nassau County (New York Times, November 17, 1974, p. 3).

Concluding Comments

In the last two sections, two interesting applications of n-person game theory were discussed. These two solutions should be viewed as illustrations of the different uses to which game-theoretic models can be put. Riker's model is a fine example of descriptive or positive theory. By bringing some elements of the model world of game theory into closer correspondence with the real world, Riker was able to deduce some testable propositions about aspects of coalition behavior. By contrast, the Shapley value and the power index have essentially a normative interpretation. They do not purport to describe or explain behavior, but rather seek to place a measure on the worth of a game to a player. Of course, the features of a game that are tapped by the Shapley value might have descriptive implications if, for example, players in voting or similar situations acted to maximize their chance of pivoting.[41] Similarly, Riker's model can also be given a normative interpretation: If a coalition seeks to maximize its payoff, it should try to reach minimal winning size.

In addition to illustrating the different ways the theory of games can be used in social analysis, these two solutions concepts, but especially the power index, also demonstrate the heuristic power of game-theoretic models. The fact that nonobvious or counterintuitive conclusions can be derived from a game-theoretic framework is perhaps the most compelling argument for coming to grips with this branch of mathematics.

NOTES

1. An informal treatment of utility theory can be found in Davis (1983: Chap. 4). A more formal discussion is given in Luce and Raiffa (1957: Chap. 2).

2. A third method of abstraction, the *characteristic function,* will be introduced in Chapter 4, when n-person games are examined.

3. In Chapter 2, a "pure" strategy will be distinguished from a "mixed" strategy. Unless otherwise noted, the terms "strategy" and "pure strategy" will be used interchangeably.

4. For some of the difficulties inherent in such an endeavor, see Rapoport's (1966: 41-43) attempt to specify the number of strategies available to each player in the simple game of tic-tac-toe.

5. Unless otherwise stated, the discussions in this book will be confined to finite games, that is, to games that terminate after a finite number of moves and have a finite number of choices available to each player at each move. For a brief summary of the theoretical structure of infinite games, see Riker and Ordeshook (1973: Chap. 8).

6. It has also been said that Napoleon advised his generals to base military decisions on this principle (Deutsch, 1978: 139).

7. The reader may wish to verify that both players in the 1914 crisis game had strictly dominant strategies (their maximin and minimax strategies respectively), but that only the Japanese had a dominant strategy (i.e., sail north) in the Battle of the Bismarck Sea.

8. The reason for the qualification will be explained shortly.

9. It is important to emphasize that this calculation is made for expository purposes only. Expected value calculations are appropriate only when each player's payoffs are measured on an interval or cardinal scale. In Figure 2.2, however, the payoffs to the players are measured only on an ordinal scale. For a discussion of the effect that different numerical payoffs that players associate with outcomes have on the calculation of mixed strategies, see Brams (1975: 20-25).

10. A more detailed discussion of this process is given by Malkevitch and Mayer (1974: 378-381). Formulas for determining optimal mixed strategies in games in which each player has only two strategies (called 2 × 2 games) are given in Kemeny et al., (1966: 368-372). For computational techniques to determine these strategies in larger games, see Luce and Raiffa (1957: Appendix 6).

11. Since either player can ensure the value of the game by using an optimal mixed strategy, a player is not hurt by selecting a nonoptimal strategy if the opponent selects an optimal strategy. Still, he or she is also not helped by switching to a nonoptimal strategy.

12. For some evidence that players approximate the use of optimal mixed strategies, see Davenport (1960) and Moore (1957). For some other criticisms and defenses of minimax and maximin strategies in zero-sum games, see Ellsberg (1956), Koo (1959), Aumann and Maschler (1972), and Davis (1974).

13. For a review of some of these solution concepts, see Luce and Raiffa (1957: Chap. 5), or Riker and Ordeshook (1973: Chap. 8).

14. The lack of any equilibrium outcome in many interactive situations may pose more of an obstacle to a satisfactory explanation of social behavior than the possible existence of multiple equilibria. Recent work by public choice theorists, for example, indicates that instability is the rule, and stability the exception, in majority-rule voting systems. For a useful collection of articles on this and related issues, see Ordeshook and Shepsle (1982).

15. A provocative discussion of other economic as well as business games can be found in McDonald (1975). For a discussion of oligopoly theory in a game-theoretic context, see Shubik (1959a), and Friedman (1977).

16. The rationale for this tactic will be further elucidated later in this chapter.

17. This assumption is not necessary for the subsequent analysis. Any other ranking that maintains the dominance relation between Liddy's two strategies produces a strategically equivalent game.

18. For the sake of simplicity, masculine pronouns will be used to refer to the prisoners and the players of the game Prisoners' Dilemma.

19. The reader will recall that Chicken is defined by the order $T > R > S > P$. The ordering in Prisoners' Dilemma merely reverses the ranking of the two worst outcomes of each player in Chicken.

20. Antitrust laws reflect the fact that at times a society may benefit from the noncooperative behavior of *some* of its members and, consequently, have an incentive to create or maintain the conditions that underlie the dilemma of the prisoners to benefit *other* members.

21. The concept of a nonmyopic equilibrium should be distinguished from the standard equilibrium concept due to Nash (1951). According to Nash, an outcome is an equilibrium if no single player benefits by unilaterally switching to another strategy. Up to this point, all references to the term "equilibrium outcome" have been to Nash's definition. Unless noted otherwise, this usage will be continued in the remainder of this essay.

22. The effect of move limitations on the long-term stability of outcomes in 2×2 games is explored in Zagare (1984).

23. Iterated games in which the last game occurs with some random probability known to the players are usually referred to as "stochastic games." For a discussion of Prisoners' Dilemma played under these conditions, see Hill (1975).

24. The analysis of the payoffs to players in a repeated game requires that the sum of the payoffs of each component game be finite. Such is the case if discounting is assumed (Taylor, 1976: 29-30). For a discussion of other assumptions that imply a finite payoff to players in a repeated game situation, see Harris (1969) and Rapoport (1967).

25. For a discussion of some of these models and their limitations, see Young (1975) and Zagare (1983b).

26. For a justification of this ranking, see Zagare (1979, 1982). Also see Thakur (1982) for alternate interpretations.

27. To simplify the representation, the abbreviation for an alternative (a) has been dropped in this and subsequent representations of this game.

28. Sophisticated strategies do not always lead to the selection of a single outcome. When they do, the game is said to be *determinate*. In determinate games, the sophisticated outcome is always an equilibrium outcome. More generally, Nash (1951) has proved that all n-person games have at least one pure or mixed strategy equilibrium outcome. As in two-person games, however, multiple equilibria may exist. And like equilibria in two-person games, equilibria in n-person games are not necessarily equivalent or interchangeable.

29. For a survey of cooperative game theory, see Luce and Raiffa (1957) or Young (1975).

30. Shubik (1968, 6: 69) has estimated this number to be between twenty and thirty. Numerous additional solution concepts have been proposed since this estimate was made. For a survey, see Rapoport (1970), Shubik (1982), or Aumann (1967).

31. Economists have been particularly interested in the core since, as Shubik (1959b) has shown, the core is identical to Edgeworth's (1891) classic contract curve.

32. An extended argument to this effect can be found in Riker (1982).

33. Recall that the definition of the dominance relationship requires that *every* member of the effective set—here each two-player coalition—receives a better payoff in an imputation if that imputation is to dominate another imputation.

34. For a proof see Riker and Ordeshook (1973: 141-142).

35. For a brief survey, see Shubik (1982: Chap. 12).

36. Many early applications of Riker's model are contained in Groennings et al. (1970). Excellent reviews of the subsequent theoretical and empirical research can be found in Brams (1975: Chap. 6) or Abrams (1980, Chap. 7).

37. The factorial sign (!) after a number means that the number is to be multiplied by every positive integer smaller than itself. For example, $3! = 3 \times 2 \times 1 = 6$. By definition, $0! = 1$.

38. This is not to say that there are not other ways of looking at voting power. For a discussion and comparison of some other measures, see Brams (1975, 1976).

39. All of these paradoxes, as well as empirical examples of some of them, are discussed in Brams (1975, 1976).

40. For a guide to the empirical literature, see Riker and Ordeshook (1973: Chap. 6) or Brams (1975: Chap. 5).
    41. The empirical evidence for this conjecture is, at best, mixed. See, for instance, Riker (1962a).

REFERENCES

ABRAMS, R. (1980) Foundations of Political Analysis: An Introduction to the Theory of Collective Choice. New York: Columbia University Press.

AUMANN, R. J. (1967) "A survey of cooperative games without side payments," in Martin Shubik (ed.) Essays in Mathematical Economics in Honor of Oskar Morgenstern. Princeton, NJ: Princeton University Press.

———and M. MASCHLER (1972) "Some thoughts on the minimax principle." Management Science 18: 54-63.

AXELROD, R. (1981) "The emergence of cooperation among egoists." American Political Science Review 75: 306-318.

———(1980a) "Effective choice in the Prisoner's Dilemma," Journal of Conflict Resolution 24: 3-25.

———(1980b) "More effective choice in the Prisoner's Dilemma." Journal of Conflict Resolution 24: 379-403.

BACHARACH, M. (1977) Economics and the Theory of Games. Boulder, CO: Westview Press.

BANZHAF, J. F., III (1965) "Weighted voting doesn't work: a mathematical analysis." Rutgers Law Review 19: 317-343.

BOREL, E. (1924) "Sur les jeux on interviennent l'hasard et l'habilité des joueurs," in J. Herman (ed.) Théorie des Probabilités. Paris: Librairie Scientifique.

———(1921) "La théorie du jeu et les équations intégrales à noyau symétrique." Comptes Rendus de l'Académie des Sciences (Paris) 173: 1304-1308.

BRAMS, S. J. (1980) Biblical Games: A Strategic Analysis of Stories in the Old Testament. Cambridge, MA: MIT Press.

———(1976) Paradoxes in Politics: An Introduction to the Nonobvious in Political Science. New York: Free Press.

———(1975) Game Theory and Politics. New York: Free Press.

———and P. J. AFFUSO (1976) "Power and size: a new paradox." Theory and Decision 7: 29-56.

BRAMS, S. J. and M. HESSEL (1982) "Absorbing outcomes in 2 × 2 games." Behavioral Science 27: 393-401.

BRAMS, S. J. and D. WITTMAN (1981) "Nonmyopic equilibria in 2 × 2 games." Conflict Management and Peace Science 6: 39-62.

BRAMS, S. J. and F. C. ZAGARE (1981) "Double deception: two against one in three person games." Theory and Decision 13: 81-90.

———(1977) "Deception in simple voting games." Social Science Research 6: 257-272.

BUENO de MESQUITA, B. (1981) The War Trap. New Haven, CT: Yale University Press.

CAPLOW, T. (1968) Two Against One: Coalitions in Triads. Englewood Cliffs, NJ: Prentice-Hall.

COLMAN, A. M. (1982) Game Theory and Experimental Games: The Study of Strategic Interaction. Oxford: Pergamon Press.

DAVENPORT, W. (1960) "Jamaican Fishing: A Game Theory Analysis," in Papers in Caribbean Anthropology. New Haven, CT: Department of Anthropology, Yale University.

DAVIS, M. (1983) Game Theory: A Nontechnical Introduction. New York: Basic Books.

———(1974) "Some further thoughts on the minimax principle." Management Science 20: 1305-1310.

DEUTSCH, K. W. (1978) The Analysis of International Relations. Englewood Cliffs, NJ: Prentice-Hall.

DOEL, H. van den (1979) Democracy and Welfare Economics. Cambridge: Cambridge University Press.

EDGEWORTH, F. (1891) Mathematical Psychics. London: Kegan Paul.

ELLSBERG, D. (1956) "Theory of the reluctant duelist." American Economic Review 46: 909-923.

FARQUHARSON, R. (1969) Theory of Voting. New Haven, CT: Yale University Press.

FRIEDMAN, J. W. (1977) Oligopoly and the Theory of Games. Amsterdam: North-Holland.

GROENNINGS,, S. E., W. KELLEY, and M. LEISERSON [eds.] (1970) The Study of Coalition Behavior. New York: Holt, Rinehart & Winston.

HAMBURGER, H. (1979) Games as Models of Social Phenomena. San Francisco: W. H. Freeman.

HARRIS, R. J. (1969) "Note on 'Optimal Policies for the Prisoner's Dilemma.'" Psychological Review 76: 363-375.

HAYWOOD, O. G., Jr. (1954) "Military decisions and game theory." Operations Research 2: 365-385.

HILL, W. W., Jr. (1975) "Prisoner's Dilemma: a stochastic solution." Mathematics Magazine 48: 103-105.

HOWARD, N. (1971) Paradoxes of Rationality: Theory of Metagames and Political Behavior. Cambridge, MA: MIT Press.

KEMENY, J. G., J. L. SNELL, and G. L. THOMPSON (1966) Introduction to Finite Mathematics. Englewood Cliffs, NJ: Prentice-Hall.

KILGOUR, D. M. (1974) "A Shapley Value for cooperative games with quarreling," in A. Rapoport (ed.) Game Theory as a Theory of Conflict Resolution. Dordrecht, Netherlands: D. Reidel.

KOO, A.Y.C. (1959) "Recurrent objections to the minimax strategy." Review of Economics and Statistics 41: 36-41.

LUCAS, W. F. (1969) "The proof that a game may not have a solution." Transactions of the American Mathematical Society 137: 219-229.

———(1968) "A game with no solution." Bulletin of the American Mathematical Society 74: 237-239.

LUCE, R. D. and H. RAIFFA (1957) Games and Decisions: Introduction and Critical Survey. New York: Wiley.

MALKEVITCH, J. and W. MEYER (1974) Graphs, Models and Finite Mathematics. Englewood Cliffs, NJ: Prentice-Hall.

McDONALD, J. (1975) The Game of Business. Garden City, NY: Doubleday.

MOORE, O. K. (1957) "Divination: a new perspective." American Anthropologist 59: 69-74.

MUZZIO, D. (1982) Watergate Games: Strategies, Choices, Outcomes. New York: New York University Press.

NASH, J. (1951) "Non-cooperative games." Annals of Mathematics 54: 286-295.

NEUMANN, J. von (1928) "Zur Theorie des Gesellschaftsspiele." Mathematische Annalen 100: 295-320.

———and O. MORGENSTERN (1953) Theory of Games and Economics Behavior (1944). Princeton, NJ: Princeton University Press.

OLSON, M. (1965) The Logic of Collective Action. Cambridge, MA: Harvard University Press.

ORDESHOOK, P. C. and K. A. SHEPSLE [eds.] (1982) Political Equilibrium. Boston: Kluwer-Nijhoff.

The Pentagon Papers: Defense Department History of United States Decisionmaking in Vietnam [Senator Gravel Edition] (1971) 4 vols. Boston: Beacon Press.

RAPOPORT, Amnon (1967) "Optimal policies for the Prisoner's Dilemma." Psychological Review 74: 136-148.

RAPOPORT, Anatol (1970) N-Person Game Theory. Ann Arbor: University of Michigan Press.

———(1966) Two-Person Game Theory: The Essential Ideas. Ann Arbor: University of Michigan Press.

———(1958) "Various meanings of theory." American Political Science Review 52: 972-988.

———and A. M. CHAMMAH (1970) Prisoner's Dilemma: A Study in Conflict and Cooperation. Ann Arbor: University of Michigan Press.

RAPOPORT, A. and M. GUYER (1966) "A taxonomy of 2 X 2 games," in General Systems: Yearbook of the Society for General Systems Research 11: 203-214.

RIKER, W. H. (1982) Liberalism against Populism: A Confrontation Between the Theory of Democracy and the Theory of Social Choice. San Francisco: W. H. Freeman.

———(1962a) "A test of adequacy of the Power Index." Behavioral Science 4: 120-131.

———(1962b) The Theory of Political Coalitions. New Haven, CT: Yale University Press.

———and P. C. ORDESHOOK (1973) An Introduction to Positive Political Theory. Englewood Cliffs, NJ: Prentice-Hall.

RUBINSTEIN, A. (1979) "A note about the 'Nowhere Denseness' of societies having an equilibrium under majority rule." Econometrica 47: 511-514.

SCHELLING, T. C. (1966) Arms and Influence. New Haven, CT: Yale University Press.

SCHOTTER, A. and G. SCHWÖDIAUER (1980) "Economics and the theory games: a survey." Journal of Economic Literature 18: 479-527.

SHAPLEY, L. S. (1953) "A value for n-person games," in H. W. Kuhn and A. W. Tucker (eds.) Contributions to the Theory of Games, vol. 2. Princeton, NJ: Princeton University Press.

———and M. SHUBIK (1954) "A method for evaluating the distribution of power in a committee system." American Political Science Review 48: 787-792.

SHUBIK, M. (1982) Game Theory in the Social Sciences: Concepts and Solutions. Cambridge, MA: MIT Press.

———(1968) "Game theory: economic applications," in International Encyclopedia of the Social Sciences. New York: Macmillan.

———(1959a) Strategy and Market Structure: Competition, Oligopoly, and the Theory of Games. New York: John Wiley.

————(1959b) "Edgeworth Market Games," in A. W. Tucker and R. D. Luce (eds.) Contributions to the Theory of Games, vol. 4. Princeton, NJ: Princeton University Press.

SNYDER, G. H. and P. DIESING (1977) Conflict Among Nations: Bargaining, Decision Making and System Structure in International Crises. Princeton, NJ: Princeton University Press.

TAYLOR, M. (1976) Anarchy and Cooperation. London: Wiley.

THAKUR, R. C. (1982) "Tacit deception reexamined: the Geneva Conference of 1954." International Studies Quarterly 26: 127-139.

YOUNG, O. R. [ed.] (1975) Bargaining: Formal Theories of Negotiation. Urbana: University of Illinois Press.

ZAGARE, F. C. (1984) "Limited move equilibria in 2×2 games." Theory and Decision 16: 1-19.

————(1983a) "A game-theoretic evaluation of the Cease-Fire Alert Decision of 1973." Journal of Peace Research 20: 73-86.

————(1983b) "Toward a reconciliation of game theory and the theory of mutual deterrence." Presented at the Fourth Annual Meeting of the Summer Institute for the Study of Conflict Theory and International Security, Los Angeles, June 23-25.

————(1982) "Competing game-theoretic explanations: the Geneva Conference of 1954." International Studies Quarterly 26: 141-147.

————(1981) "Nonmyopic equilibria and the Middle East crisis of 1967." Conflict Management and Peace Science 5: 139-162.

————(1979) "The Geneva Conference of 1954: a case of tacit deception." International Studies Quarterly 23: 390-411.

————(1977) "A game-theoretic analysis of the Vietnam negotiations: preferences and strategies, 1968-1973." Journal of Conflict Resolution 21: 663-684.

ZERMELO. E. (1912) "Über eine Anwendung der Mengelehre auf die Theorie des Schachspiels." Proceedings of the Fifth International Congress of Mathematicians 2: 501-510.

FRANK C. ZAGARE is Assistant Professor of Political Science at Boston University. He has written numerous articles on game theory and its application to international affairs. His current research involves the development of models applicable to international crises and deterrence.

Quantitative Applications in the Social Sciences

A SAGE UNIVERSITY PAPER SERIES

$10.95 each

To order, please use order form on the next page.

Quantitative Applications in the Social Sciences

A SAGE UNIVERSITY PAPER SERIES

$10.95 each

SAGE PUBLICATIONS, INC.
P.O. BOX 5084
THOUSAND OAKS, CALIFORNIA 91359-9924